People Styles at Work

Making Bad Relationships Good and Good Relationships Better

Robert Bolton and
Dorothy Grover Bolton

American Management Association

New York • Atlanta • Boston • Chicago • Kansas City • San Francisco • Washington, D. C.
Brussels • Mexico City • Tokyo • Toronto

This book is available at a special
discount when ordered in bulk quantities.
For information, contact Special Sales Department,
AMACOM, a division of American Management Association,
1601 Broadway, New York, NY 10019.

Library of Congress Cataloging-in-Publication Data

Bolton, Robert.
    People styles at work : making bad relationships good and good
relationships better / Robert Bolton and Dorothy Grover Bolton.
        p.   cm.
    Includes bibliographical references and index.
    ISBN-10: 0-8144-7723-2
    ISBN-13: 978-0-8144-7723-6
    1. Psychology, Industrial.   2. Interpersonal relations.
3. Interpersonal communication.   I. Bolton, Dorothy Grover,
II. Title.
HF5548.8.B634   1996
158.7—dc20   96-6109
                                                       CIP

Printing number

29

To Our Fathers

Walter Alexander Bolton, my dad. Your love nurtured me; your independence emboldens me; your integrity inspires me.

Walter Grover, whose excellence in manufacturing set the standard for his industry and whose excellence as a person set the standard for his family.

Contents

Foreword   vii

Introduction   ix

Part One: Understanding People   **1**

1. No Wonder We Have People Problems   3
2. People Are More Predictable Than You Think   8
3. What's Your Style?   13
4. Two Keys to Understanding People   16
5. Seeing Yourself as Others See You   24
6. Four Paths to Success   28
7. Styles Under Stress   47

**Part Two: Style Flex: The Key to Productive
Relationships**   **63**

8. Finding Common Ground With People   65
9. Four Steps to Better Relationships   72
10. How to Identify a Person's Style   80
11. Too Much of a Good Thing   89
12. Flexing in Special Situations   99
13. Three Keys to Good Relationships   110

Appendix I   For *Amiables* Only: How to Flex to
                  Each Style   121

Appendix II   For *Drivers* Only: How to Flex to
                  Each Style   136

Appendix III   For *Expressives* Only: How to Flex to
                  Each Style   154

Appendix IV   For *Analyticals* Only: How to Flex to
                Each Style   170

Notes   188

Index   191

Foreword

In an era when organizations of every kind are asking employees to do more with less, the quality of your working relationships is more important than ever. Helping you improve the quality of these relationships is what this book is all about. It won't happen overnight, but as you apply the ideas within these pages you'll find that you're more effective with your co-workers. And as the *way* you work together improves, you'll get more done in less time with less effort. The goal of this book is to give you the tools to get in sync with others—and make your life easier in the process.

The beauty of *People Styles at Work* is its how-to nature. As behavioral scientists and experts in interpersonal communication, Bob and Dot Bolton and their colleagues at Ridge Associates have spent over twenty years researching, testing, applying, and teaching the methods you'll find here. The book is divided into two parts. Part One explains a model that enables you to gain crucial insights into yourself and the many people you interact with in the course of a day. Part Two provides step-by-step guidelines for *applying* those insights, allowing you to create more pleasant and productive relationships. There are four appendixes that give highly specific suggestions about what you can do to relate better to different types of people.

As CEO of Ridge Associates, Inc.—and the Boltons' son—I am proud to introduce you to *People Styles at Work*. As you apply what you read, you'll find that you are developing better relationships with the people you work with—and the people you live with.

As with anything that requires behavior change, the hardest part is staying with your new skills until they become habitual. We designed the following supplemental materials to make that challenge a little easier:

1. The "People Styles Planner," a worksheet that helps you track your progress applying the concepts of this book over a six-week span—the amount of time it takes to acquire a new skill.
2. "Opposites Do Attract," an article that applies people styles to the challenges of love relationships.

To receive either or both, please write, call, or e-mail Ridge Associates.
We will gladly send them to you free of charge.

Mailing Address:	Ridge Associates, Inc.
	5 Ledyard Avenue
	Cazenovia, NY 13035
Phone number:	(315) 655-3393
E-mail address:	info@ridge.com

Enjoy the book—and the relationships it can help you create.

Jim Bolton
Ridge Conference Center
Cazenovia, New York

Introduction

Success at work and happiness in life depend in large measure on your ability to relate well to others. Yet it's not easy to have consistently good relationships with everyone you interact with: co-workers, customers, suppliers, family, friends, neighbors, and acquaintances. Some people, though, are better than others at creating and maintaining relationships. But even these individuals find that "people problems" bedevil their lives. Chances are that anyone can be much more effective at work and enjoy life more fully by finding better ways of relating to people.

People Differences Lead to People Problems

Differences between people are a major source of friction. For example, our colleague Michelle does everything at a rapid-fire pace. She walks fast, talks fast, and decides fast. She finishes projects in a hurry. As luck would have it, Michelle is often teamed with John, who is very deliberate. John walks slowly, talks slowly, and decides slowly. He is slow in completing projects. Though these differences may not seem like a big deal, if they aren't managed well they're likely to erode Michelle and John's working relationship. You've undoubtedly seen how differences like these can undermine your relationships, hamper your performance, and add needless stress to your life.

Fortunately, it's possible to manage such differences so work relationships are enhanced, productivity is increased, and there's more richness and spice to life. You can make these differences work *for*, not against, you. Although this book focuses on improving work relationships, the concepts can be applied to interactions with anyone.

The number and variety of differences between people is overwhelming. It's not possible for human beings to adapt to all the individual characteristics of all the people they meet in the course of a typical day. Carl Jung, one of the towering figures of modern psychology, sought a manageable way of dealing with human differences. His *Psychological Types*, which was published in 1921, described four types of people: Thinkers,

Feelers, Intuiters, and Sensors. To oversimplify a bit, if a person you are working with is a Thinker and you are a Feeler, then you can determine what you can do to make it more comfortable for him or her to work with you. A problem with Jung's model is that as a *psychological* model it was about people's *inner states,* rather than their outer behaviors, making it difficult to identify another person's style. The Myers-Briggs model, based on Jung's work, suffers from the same deficit.

About forty years after the publication of Jung's *Psychological Types,* Dr. David Merrill, an industrial psychologist, developed an approach that focused on differences between people's *outer behaviors* rather than on differences in their inner states. Merrill used the newly available computer technology and a recently developed statistical technique to group people into four styles. There are many similarities between Merrill's styles and Jung's types. Merrill's model, however, was for most applications by far the more practical of the two, since it was based on behaviors that are directly observable. What this meant was that with a little instruction, the average person could objectively identify another person's style. It created a very useful way of "reading" other people and relating to them more effectively.

This way of improving work relationships is based primarily on Merrill's work, although there are important differences. A more detailed explanation of this approach to working with others is given in the following chapters. For now, it's enough to say:

- There are four styles of people, none of which is better or worse than any of the other styles.
- Each style has characteristic strengths and weaknesses not shared by the other styles.
- Each person has a dominant style that influences the way he or she works.
- Our population is evenly divided among the four styles.
- People of each style can be successful.
- The behavioral patterns of one style tend to trigger stress in the other three styles.
- To create optimum working relationships, it's necessary to get in sync with the style-based behavioral patterns of the people you are working with.

Whether at work or at home, success and happiness involve relating to others across a chasm of significant behavioral differences. Clearly, if you could figure out how to bridge the gap between yourself and others, you could make your own life—and theirs—much easier, happier, and more productive. That in a nutshell is what this book is about.

Figure I-1. Different styles can produce the same favorable results.

A Look Ahead

Part One of this book provides a pragmatic understanding of yourself and others. It doesn't delve into esoteric psychological theory. Instead, it provides a straightforward, practical explanation of what you need to know to relate effectively to others.

Chapter One identifies some of the general differences between the styles and how these differences can lead to people problems as you interact with those who are important to your success and happiness. On the other hand, when handled skillfully, these same differences can create increased productivity and more vital relationships.

Chapter Two explains that even though people may react differently than you, you can usually figure out how to relate effectively to them. Chapter Three helps you capture data for understanding your own style. Chapter Four presents two dimensions of behavior that are keys to understanding yourself and others. With this background, in Chapter Five you complete your assessment of how you come across to other people. Each of the four styles is portrayed in Chapter Six, with crucial distinctions between styles spelled out. Chapter Seven shows how people of each style tend to react to excessive stress.

Part Two shows how to build more productive relationships by applying the knowledge of yourself and others gained in Part One. Chapter Eight introduces you to "style flex," a way of creating common ground with people very different from yourself. Style flex is the intriguing ability to be truly yourself while relating on another person's wavelength.

The four steps involved in flexing to another person's style are described in Chapter Nine. In Chapter Ten, you learn how to identify a person's style. Most people overdo aspects of their style to the point where they stress others and undermine their own effectiveness, so in Chapter Eleven you find ways to increase your effectiveness by decreasing excessive or inappropriate expressions of your style. Chapter Twelve coaches you on how to make style flex work in challenging situations.

The book has four very important appendixes, one for each of the four styles. Here you find specific guidelines on how you can flex to persons of each style.

Acknowledgments

We're grateful to the board of directors of Ridge Associates, Inc., headquartered in Cazenovia, New York, for freeing us from other responsibilities so that we could concentrate on writing this book.

Through the years many people have helped us arrive at a deeper understanding of styles.

Workshop participants gave us both examples and questions that forced us to greater clarity and helped us make the model more pragmatic. We've worked with a cadre of trainers through the years who have provided us with new ways of seeing and phrasing things. We're also indebted to scores of applied behavioral scientists whose research and writing provided strong underpinnings for this book.

In addition to all these people who contributed to our knowledge of styles, we owe special words of thanks to a handful of people.

Kristin and Jim Bolton (our daughter and son), who are able colleagues with a good understanding of people styles, made suggestions that improved each chapter. They added ideas, suggested deletions and sharpened the phrasing throughout.

Two other longtime friends and associates of ours at Ridge were also invaluable in the writing of this book. Liz Smyth cheerfully and thoughtfully word-processed draft after draft of each chapter. Liz has a fine sense of language, and on virtually every page of the manuscript she suggested alternative phrasings, most of which were retained. Once the early drafts were finished, Wilma Brownback entered the scene with her copyediting skills and carefully honed the final product. Along with precise use of words and mastery of grammar, Wilma brought to the project an archivist's awareness of all the resources that had been developed for our workshops through the years.

Andrea Pedolsky, the editor at AMACOM who suggested this project, was a strong source of support and encouragement. Mary Glenn, who succeeded Andrea, picked up the project in midstream and saw it through to completion.

Developmental editors Anne Basye and Jacqueline Flynn made significant improvements to the manuscript, and copy editor Tom Finnegan fine-tuned the manuscript. After all this work, issues that remained were worked through with associate editor Richard Gatjens whose skill and sensitivity are greatly appreciated.

Thanks, folks, for all your help.

Part One

Understanding People

I could save myself a lot of wear and tear with people if I just learned to understand them.

—Ralph Ellison, in *The Writer's Craft,* John Hersey, ed.

Chapter One

No Wonder We Have People Problems

As long as you live, you'll have at least some unwelcome and unproductive friction with others. There are difficulties to be worked through even in the best relationships. In more troubled relationships, people problems may loom large enough to seriously undermine both morale and productivity. Of all the problems we face in life, people problems are generally the toughest to solve. Difficult as task problems may be, most of us would choose them over people problems. Besides, when a task problem is especially difficult to handle, it's usually so because one or more painful people problems are embedded in it.

People problems tend to take the greatest toll on us personally; they produce significant emotional wear and tear. They disturb our sleep. Too often, people problems drag on endlessly and get worse, not better, over time. Obviously, differences between people aren't the only sources of interpersonal tension. They are, however, a major factor in much misunderstanding and conflict.

It's no wonder everyone has people problems. Behavioral science researchers have discovered that 75 percent of the population is significantly different from you. These people, many of whom are important to your success:

- Think differently
- Decide differently
- Use time differently
- Work at a different pace
- Communicate differently
- Handle emotions differently
- Manage stress differently
- Deal with conflicting opinions differently

Not necessarily worse. Not necessarily better. But differently. Behaviorally speaking, you're in the minority. Every individual is.

As you can imagine, at work there are problems associated with your being so different from most of your colleagues. Social psychologists have found that people who are very different from one another:

- Have a harder time establishing rapport
- Miscommunicate more often
- Are less likely to be persuasive with one another
- Rub each other the wrong way—just by being themselves

These facts help explain why it's quite a stretch for you to work effectively with many of your colleagues. It takes some doing to get on their wavelength. The more you think about it, the less surprising it is that everyone has people problems at work.

Spencer Noblock[1] learned this the hard way. Spencer had had an excellent working relationship with Jan White, his manager, for more than three years. Then Jan was transferred. Spencer didn't hit it off nearly as well with Bill Freed, his new manager. It wasn't that Bill was unreasonable; he was well-liked by most employees. Spencer was puzzled. Why wasn't he able to work as smoothly with Bill as he had with Jan?

Spencer was a conscientious manager who believed detailed information was essential to good decision making. He loved it when his employees really did their homework and then filled him in on the nitty-gritty of their work. That was his way of staying on top of what was happening in his department. Naturally, Spencer wanted in like manner to provide his new manager with the best information available. Because Spencer so appreciated detailed communication, he diligently covered all the fine points of each project.

Spencer became troubled that in their weekly meetings Bill was increasingly nervous. He noticed a recurring sequence: Bill seemed to get on edge when Spencer reported on a project; then Bill would chain smoke—more than was customary for him. Soon, he'd pace about the room, appearing impatient and distracted. Clearly, Bill was frustrated by something Spencer was doing, but Spencer couldn't figure out what. After all, Bill needed to know what was happening in Spencer's department. And Spencer was giving him the same kinds of reports that had so pleased Jan, his previous manager.

At times, Bill told Spencer, "Just give me the big picture on this one. I trust you've done your usual thorough job on it."

Spencer, though, would have been uncomfortable giving what seemed to be a less than adequate briefing and so continued his thorough presentations. After all, that's what he would have wanted if he were in Bill's shoes.

The problem, of course, was that Spencer wasn't in Bill's shoes. Bill was. Bill's working style was very different from Spencer's. Even when

Spencer saw that his way of meeting with Bill was disconcerting to Bill, he clung rigidly to his typical way of interacting. Because neither adapted to the other, their working relationship continued to deteriorate.

When people's ways of working don't mesh well, their stress goes up and productivity goes down. You've undoubtedly found yourself in this plight at times since it's a statistical probability that three of four people are very different from you. Such people differences inevitably exist among many of your co-workers.

Other People Are Crucial to Your Success and Happiness

In nearly every area of life, other people are crucial to your success and happiness. People who relate well to others have a more rewarding and happier life in all facets of their experience.

There's hardly a job today where you're not expected to excel in working with people. Societal analysts say we've moved from an industrial to a service economy. What that means in practical terms is that work today is far more people-intensive. Virtually every position involves more contact with people than a few decades ago. *The ability to relate well to people has become a critical factor for success in nearly every position in the modern organization.*

Working with people has always been seen as a prime responsibility of executives and managers. Since supervisors, managers, and executives have several people reporting to them, their most crucial asset is the ability to achieve productivity through others. In recent years, the people part of the manager's job has grown far more difficult. Much that could once be achieved by *authority* now has to be accomplished through *influence.* Managers are expected to empower others, encourage participation, and function increasingly as effective team players. And all this needs to be done in a workforce that's becoming more and more diverse.

A nonprofit research institute studied twenty-one derailed executives—individuals who, based on their early successes, had been expected to go much higher in the organization but whose progress stalled or careers ended when they were fired or forced to retire early. The derailed executives were compared with a group of "arrivers" who made it to the top. These two groups of talented managers showed many similarities and only a few differences. One dissimilarity, however, stood out; as the researchers reported, "Ability—or inability—to understand other people's perspectives was the most glaring difference between the derailed and the arrivers. Only 25 percent of the derailed were described as having a special ability with people; among the arrivers, the figure was 75 percent."[2]

In today's workplace, individual contributors and frontline employees also need to excel at working with people. Virtually all the major trends of organizational life require everyone to be competent at building productive work relationships. We've clearly entered an era in which the ability to relate effectively to people is of prime importance in nearly every position in the workplace.

Just as a major factor in success is one's ability to work well with people, the chief cause of failure in all types of work is unsatisfactory relationships. Research aimed at discovering the primary reason for the termination of employees has provided surprisingly consistent results for decades. Most studies have found that, aside from decisions to downsize, about 80 percent of employee firings are due to poor interpersonal relationships.

Making the Differences Work *for* You
Rather Than Against You

Problems can be opportunities in disguise. Although it may be challenging to work with someone very different from yourself, you can make that difficulty work *for* you rather than against you.

There's always a competitive advantage to mastering an ability that's in high demand and short supply. If you learn to work productively with all types of people, you'll be far more valuable to your employer. As a management trainee from a Fortune 500 agribusiness said at the conclusion of a workshop, "I always thought I was good with people, but this way of working with people gives me the edge."

There's another way that people differences can be made to work for you. We all have different gifts. No one can be outstanding at everything. You frequently need to supplement your own abilities with the strengths of people very different from yourself. As you become expert at teaming with people whose skills complement yours, you become a stronger and more versatile contributor.

That's what eventually happened with Spencer. He finally realized that he needed to come up with a different way of relating to his manager. Spencer eventually remembered hearing someone say that people have different working styles, and that to function well with another person you need to understand that person's style and how it's different from your own. Then you figure out how to get in sync with the other person's way of working. Since there was no place for the relationship to go but up, Spencer tried the new strategy. He eliminated much of the detail from his reports and stepped up the pace of his conversations with Bill. Spencer's greater adaptability immediately decreased the interpersonal tension and brought about a better working relationship.

According to Spencer, within a year his working relationship with

Bill became even more productive than it had been with Jan. "Jan and I got a lot done, but we were too much alike," he said. "Bill often has a different perspective on things than I have. He's more people-oriented and much faster-paced than I am. That balances my task-focused, detail-oriented approach. Now that we've learned to work together, we're great at selling proposals to top management and getting more cooperation from other divisions. When my technical and administrative skills are combined with Bill's networking ability, we're some team."

If you want to work productively with people very different from yourself, it helps to be able to predict how they're apt to do things and how they like to be treated. In Chapter Two you'll see that people are more predictable than you might think.

Chapter Two

People Are More Predictable Than You Think

Ever been baffled by someone's reaction to something you've said or done? Join the club.

Perhaps you've acted with the very best of intentions only to learn that what you did irritated the other person. It's disheartening to be ambushed by negative reactions you didn't expect and don't think you deserve.

Such experiences lead many to throw up their hands in despair at ever being able to understand people. It's a widespread opinion that "there's no predicting other people."

If that were true, it would be bad news indeed. The reason? Prediction is a major determinant of behavior.

In virtually *every* venture, your behavior is largely shaped by the predictions you make. When you decide something, you predict that the option chosen will be more satisfying than others you considered. When you make a change, you predict that the new condition will ultimately be more favorable than the old one. Prediction influences even our relatively insignificant actions. You turn on a faucet because you predict water will be released. You turn a doorknob and pull because you predict that these actions will open the door.

It would be an oversimplification to say that prediction is the only factor that shapes behavior. Instinct plays a role, as does the unconscious. Habit has its impact, too. Nonetheless, prediction plays a major role in determining what we do—and what we avoid doing.

People Are Surprisingly Predictable

Fortunately, human behavior isn't nearly as random as it often seems. Behavioral scientists have found that it's much more predictable than most people realize. Think, for example, of opinion polling. On November 4, 1980, before anyone voted, Hamilton Jordan—who ran Jimmy Carter's reelection campaign for president—was handed the results of a last-minute poll that foretold a lopsided loss for Carter. Jordan commented, "What a funny feeling, I thought. Not a single person in the country has voted and we already know we've been defeated."[1] The outcome of the vote was just as the poll predicted—Ronald Reagan won a landslide victory. Opinion polls show a remarkable ability to predict voting behavior.

One of the more interesting studies about human predictability comes from psychologist Arnold Mandell. Through careful observation of National Football League (NFL) players, Mandell found that certain behaviors were strongly linked to other, quite different characteristics. When he saw evidence of some of these behaviors, he would predict with considerable accuracy that the player would have the characteristics he thought were associated. In time, he got to the point where he could predict a lot about an NFL player just by looking at his locker. When Mandell saw a clean locker, he would assume, usually correctly, that the player was on the offensive team, liked structure and discipline, enjoyed the repetitious practice of well-designed plays, and was rather conservative. When he saw a messy locker he predicted that the player was almost certainly on the defensive team, disliked structure, was liable to challenge rules and regulations, and would be much more difficult to manage than his counterparts on the offensive team.

Mandell was able to predict with much accuracy because he created a sound model to guide him. Opinion polls, which show a remarkable ability to predict behavior, are also based on models that aid prediction. A model is a "tool for the mind," to use a phrase coined in the seventeenth century by Francis Bacon, one of the early figures of modern science.

An elegant model is a useful simplification of reality. It enables you to ignore a mass of irrelevant or less relevant details so you can focus on what is most important. A model shows what to look for, helps identify meaningful patterns, and aids in interpreting what you see. In other words, a model helps cut through the distracting aspects of a situation so you can better grasp the essence of what you want to understand.

If models can be so useful in predicting how people will act, why not create a model to forecast how specific types of people are likely to behave and want to be treated in the everyday situations that make up our lives? The Social Style Model™ was developed to do just that. We think you'll be amazed at the model's helpfulness as you learn and use it to create better working relationships.

A little more than three decades ago, Dr. David Merrill, an industrial psychologist, developed the Social Style Model, which is the basis for our approach to PeopleStyles. There are many such models that are designed to do the same thing—help people better understand and better relate to others who are different from themselves. On many counts we think this is the best model for use in the business environment. After two decades of using it, teaching it to others, and doing extensive research on it and its competitors, we're more convinced than ever of the viability of the basic model. At the same time, we and our colleagues have developed enhancements that we think make it even more effective.

What's a style? Simply put, *your style is the way other people see you behave.* You'll understand the model better, though, if we use a fuller definition:

> A person's style is his or her pattern of assertive and responsive behavior. The pattern is useful in predicting how the person prefers to work with others.

Let's look at some of the key elements of this definition.

Behavior

This approach to understanding people is distinguished from many others in that it focuses on behavior, not on personality. Behavior is what a person does; it's the *outer* expression of a person's life.

In other words, this model is about *body language*. How fast does the person walk? How much does he or she gesture? How loudly does the person speak? How much inflection does he or she use?

It's also about the *words a person chooses*. Is the person more likely to ask your opinion or tell his or her point of view? Is the conversation centered more on task or on relationship?

By contrast, one's *personality* includes mental and emotional as well as behavioral characteristics. It deals as much with the inner self as with the outer expression of a person's life.

This model doesn't dabble in the inner realm of thoughts, attitudes, feelings, and values. It doesn't encourage users to probe into the psyche of the individuals they are working with. Instead, it teaches people how to understand the behavior that's there for everyone to see.

Patterns

A person's style is based on patterns of behavior. A pattern is a group of traits that form a coherent, integrated whole. An understanding of styles is possible because certain behaviors go together. The behaviors associated with a pattern are linked and have a thematic consistency.

It's not enough to understand each isolated behavior. You need to sense the patterns to understand the person. Learned Hand, the renowned federal judge, stated, "A man's life, like a piece of tapestry, is made up of many strands which, interwoven, make a pattern. To separate a single one and look at it alone not only destroys the whole, but gives the strand itself a false value."

When you note a person using some behaviors of a pattern, you can assume that other behaviors are present that are part of that same pattern. Like Mandell, you can predict behavioral characteristics not observed based on some behaviors you have observed. The understanding of patterns is so important that Marilyn Ferguson, author of *The Aquarian Conspiracy* and editor of the *Brain/Mind Bulletin*, says, "The greatest learning disability of all may be pattern blindness—the inability to see relationships or detect meaning."[2]

Habit

One's style is determined by *habitual* rather than occasional behaviors. It's about the things a person does over and over again, day after day, for the umpteenth time. It's about the things we do without consciously thinking. Habitual actions are called "second nature" because we rely on them almost instinctively—such as hitting the brakes when the car in front of us suddenly slows down. Because behaviors associated with our style are so habitual, they feel natural. We feel at home with them. That's why our style is often referred to as our "comfort zone."

Even in our relationships with other people, much of our behavior is habitual. Obviously, people aren't robots doing exactly the same behavior again and again. Rather, they do the same *type* of behavior repeatedly.

Skeptical? Many people are. But think about it. Don't the people in your department have behavioral tendencies that just about everyone is aware of? For example, as you read the following list, mentally fill in each blank with the name of a specific individual who matches these descriptions:

_____ is usually late for appointments and meetings.
_____ is nearly always punctual.
_____ tends to be very thorough.
_____ keeps touching base with people.
_____ has a story for nearly every occasion.
_____ is a no-nonsense, "just do it" kind of person.

Much of our behavior remains fairly consistent from one situation to another. It's this consistency that makes it possible to predict how people are likely to behave in the future.

Predicting Probable Behavior

When we affirm that people are fairly predictable, we're not suggesting you'll be able to foretell someone's every move. Nor do we claim you can know for sure how a person will react. *When we're dealing with people, there are no certainties—but there are probabilities.* By probable, we mean more likely than not. Thus when we make predictions about people, we avoid words such as "whenever," "always," or "never." We rely on "usually," "frequently," "tends to," "is likely to," "seldom," and so forth. In the following pages we generally omit these qualifiers for the sake of readability; but do understand that we're talking about probabilities rather than certainties.

Some people are unimpressed with predictions that are only probabilities. They seek something more definite. However, when it comes to anticipating how a given person will react, you can never be absolutely sure.

We're grateful for this degree of uncertainty. Without it, without spontaneity in our relationships with others, much of the joy of living would be forfeited. Furthermore, if everyone went through life with robotlike, preprogrammed predictability, we would lose one of our priceless gifts: human freedom.

We think you'll enjoy the improvements you can make in relationships when you are guided by strong probabilities. As James Thurber realized, "A pinch of probability is worth a pound of perhaps."

In Chapter Four, we begin presenting the specifics of this model for predicting the behavior of others. Before getting into that material, though, you have an inventory in Chapter Three that helps you identify your own style.

Chapter Three

What's Your Style?

Self-knowledge is the beginning of wisdom. The focus of this chapter is a Behavioral Inventory that can help you figure out your style. This is the all-important first step for improving your working relationships.

How Other People See You

Your style is *not* based on how *you* see yourself. Your style is based on *other people's* perceptions of you—regardless of how much or how little those perceptions match your own self-image. In filling out the Behavioral Inventory, read each item from the standpoint of the way you think *other people* perceive you. It may help to select three people you work with and try to see yourself through their eyes as you take the inventory.

There are no good or bad styles; there are only differences between people. Success or failure is unrelated to any style. On the inventory, there are no good or bad choices—no right or wrong answers.

However, each of us has a picture of how we'd *like* to be seen by other people. Because we're human, there's always some disparity between our daily actions and the way we hope others perceive us. Discipline yourself to be as objective as possible. Select those items that to the best of your knowledge reflect the way others experience you.

Behavioral Inventory Guidelines

As you take this inventory, remember that your style is how you are perceived by *others*. The inventory gives you eighteen pairs of statements, each with a box. Choose the statement in each pair that you think most accurately expresses how other people see you. Sometimes you may think neither of the statements reflects how you come across to others. Nevertheless, choose the statement you think *more closely describes* how others perceive your behavior. On some items you may think some people would see you as described by one statement while others might think of you as described by the other statement. For those items, select the statement that represents how a majority might view you (even a small majority of 51 percent).

Each inventory item has a word in it that suggests a comparison: *more, less, fewer, softer, louder, slower, quicker,* and so forth. You may wonder, "More than what?" "Louder than what?" In each case, think in terms of "more than," "less than," "louder than" *half the population.*

Indicate your choice by drawing an X in the box to the left of the statement in each pair that better describes how you think others see you. In the example below, if you think "less use of hands when talking" is a more accurate statement of how you come across than "more use of hands when talking," mark an X in the box connected by the dotted line to the first statement.

❑........................ Less use of hands when talking
❑ .... More use of hands when talking

Behavioral Inventory

Be sure to select one statement from each of the pairs. Be sure to put the X in the correct box.

1. ❑........................ More likely to lean backward when stating opinions
    ❑ .... More likely to be erect or lean forward when stating opinions

2.   ❑......... Less use of hands when talking
         ❑ ... More use of hands when talking

3. ❑........................ Demonstrates less energy
    ❑ .... Demonstrates more energy

4.   ❑......... More controlled body movement
         ❑ ... More flowing body movement

5. ❑........................ Less forceful gestures
    ❑ .... More forceful gestures

6.   ❑......... Less facial expressiveness
         ❑ ... More facial expressiveness

7. ❑........................ Softer-spoken
    ❑ .... Louder voice

8.   ❑.......... Appears more serious
                 ❑ ... Appears more fun-loving

9.   ❑....................... More likely to ask questions
        ❑ .... More likely to make statements

10.   ❑.......... Less inflection in voice
                 ❑ ... More inflection in voice

11.   ❑....................... Less apt to exert pressure for action
        ❑ .... More apt to exert pressure for action

12.   ❑.......... Less apt to show feelings
                 ❑ ... More apt to show feelings

13.   ❑....................... More tentative when expressing opinions
        ❑ .... Less tentative when expressing opinions

14.   ❑.......... More task-oriented conversations
                 ❑ ... More people-oriented conversations

15.   ❑....................... Slower to resolve problem situations
        ❑ .... Quicker to resolve problem situations

16.   ❑.......... More oriented toward facts and logic
                 ❑ ... More oriented toward feelings and opinions

17.   ❑....................... Slower-paced
        ❑ .... Faster-paced

18.   ❑.......... Less likely to use small-talk or tell anecdotes
                 ❑ ... More likely to use small-talk and tell anecdotes

— — — —   Total Scores

Interpreting the Inventory

Although it's best to *complete* the Behavioral Inventory before you've learned much about PeopleStyles, it's best to wait on *interpreting* the results of the inventory until after you know more about the model. So we'll hold off for several pages before showing you how to calculate your style from the inventory. Your style is based on two dimensions of behavior. We describe those crucial variables in Chapter Four.

Chapter Four

Two Keys to Understanding People

Throughout history there has been no dearth of methods attempting to help us understand other people. However, most of the methods were fundamentally inaccurate, or they were too complex and unwieldy to be used by the average person. Another difficulty was that there were often dozens or even hundreds of characteristics to keep track of.

Two Dimensions of Behavior

The genius of the PeopleStyles approach is that it focuses on just two dimensions of behavior. Only *two*! Out of the welter of signals issuing from another person, you only have to observe two clusters of behavior to ascertain that person's behavioral style.

How is it possible to reduce hundreds of variables to just two and still be able to predict other people's behavior? A key to this breakthrough was the discovery that certain types of behaviors tend to be linked to each other in clusters of traits, called syndromes.

In the 1960s, Dr. David Merrill discovered that two clusters of behavior—assertiveness and responsiveness—are incredibly helpful in predicting how other people are apt to behave. These key dimensions of behavior combine to form the Social Style grid, portrayed in Figure 4–1.

Assertiveness

In this model, *one's level of assertiveness is the degree to which one's behaviors are seen by others as being forceful or directive.* It's helpful to think of a continuum of assertiveness. The gradations of behavior along the continuum are imperceptible, as indicated by the gradual darkening of the assertiveness continuum as you look from left to right in Figure 4–2.

At this point, we're only concerned about whether a person's behav-

Figure 4–1. The Social Style grid.

ior is typically more assertive or less assertive than that of half the population. The assertiveness continuum in Figure 4–2 is cut in half by a line or axis (the responsiveness continuum seen in Figure 4–1). People whose characteristic behavior is more assertive than half of the population are sometimes referred to as "right of the line" because that's where they are located on the continuum. People in the less assertive half of the continuum get their needs met by using a less forceful and less directive manner than do half of the population. We speak of them as "left of the line."

A distinction is often made between assertiveness and aggressiveness. It's a significant difference. However, in terms of this model, the difference between highly assertive behavior and aggressive behavior is irrelevant. All you need to know is whether or not a person's behavior is more or less forceful and directive than that of half the population. Aggressive behavior is an indicator of *use* of style—not of what the person's style is.

Figure 4–2. The assertiveness continuum.

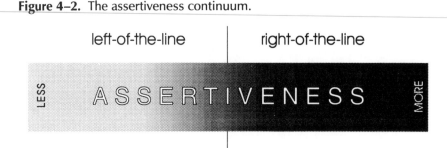

Regarding the other half of the continuum, people sometimes assume that lower levels of assertiveness indicate submissiveness. Not so. While it's true that some less assertive people are submissive, many simply use less forceful ways to get their needs met. *In relation to a person's style,* the difference between less assertive behavior and submissive behavior is irrelevant. All you need to know is whether that person's behavior *appears* less forceful and directive than it does for half the population. *Submissive behavior is an indicator of how people use their style—not what their style is.*

When we say someone is less assertive or more assertive, we don't mean he or she is always that way. Some behaviors of a less assertive person may be forceful. Some behaviors of a more assertive person may be less directive. Most of a person's behaviors, however, will fall within a fairly limited area of the continuum. People often think they move along the assertion continuum rather freely. But we're creatures of habit, and that's rarely the case.

Bear in mind that for our purposes assertiveness refers to a person's *behavior.* One's level of assertiveness, as perceived by other people, does not necessarily reflect a person's level of inner drive.

Many less assertive people have a strong inner drive, but their typical behavior would not be perceived as forceful or directive. They get their needs met in a manner that's softer and quieter than that of their behaviorally assertive colleagues. The phrase *an iron hand in a velvet glove* describes the way some people's apparently understated behavior masks an underlying strong will and determination.

Recall from Chapter Three that in determining someone's People-Style, we use comparative words such as *more, less, louder, softer,* and so forth. When estimating a person's level of assertiveness, we do the same thing: We determine whether people tend to see that person as exhibiting *more* or *less* of specific patterns of behavior than half the population.

Characteristic Behaviors of More Assertive People

More assertive people have the following behavioral characteristics. Compared to less assertive people, they tend to:

- Exude more energy
- Move faster
- Gesture more vigorously
- Have more intense eye contact
- Be erect or lean forward, especially when making a point
- Speak more rapidly
- Speak louder
- Speak more often
- Address problems quicker
- Decide quicker
- Be more risk-oriented
- Be more confrontational
- Be more direct and emphatic when expressing opinions, making requests, and giving directions
- Exert more pressure for a decision or for taking action
- Demonstrate anger quicker

More assertive people have most but not necessarily all of these characteristics.

Characteristic Behaviors of Less Assertive People

Less assertive people tend to:

- Demonstrate less energy
- Move slower
- Gesture less vigorously
- Have less intense eye contact
- Lean backward even when making a point
- Speak less rapidly
- Speak more softly
- Speak less often
- Be slower to address problems
- Decide less quickly
- Be less risk-oriented
- Be less confrontational
- Be less direct and less emphatic when expressing opinions, making requests, and giving directions
- Exert less pressure for making a decision or taking action
- Demonstrate anger less quickly

People who are less assertive than half the population have most but not necessarily all of these characteristics.

Responsiveness

Responsiveness is the other crucial dimension of behavior in this model. *One's level of responsiveness is the degree to which one is seen by others as showing his or her own emotions or demonstrating awareness of the feelings of others.* The gradations of behavior along the responsiveness continuum are indicated by the gradual darkening of the continuum as you look from the top to the bottom of Figure 4–3.

At this point, we're only concerned about whether or not a person's behavior tends to be more responsive or less responsive than that of half the population. Once again, the responsiveness continuum in Figure 4–3 is cut in half by a line (the assertiveness continuum from Figure 4–1). People who are more reserved are said to be "above the line." Those who are more emotionally disclosing are referred to as "below the line."

When we say people are emotionally responsive, we don't mean they always "let it all hang out." There are times when they mute their expression of feelings, too. It's just that they're generally more emotionally de-

Figure 4–3. The responsiveness continuum.

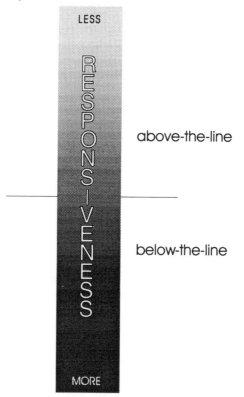

monstrative than above-the-liners. Likewise, people who are emotionally controlled sometimes let their feelings show. J. P. Morgan, the famous banker, was aloof at work and in public. At times, though, as when he read *A Christmas Carol* to his family, the normally inexpressive financier would get all choked up. So when we say someone is emotionally controlled or emotionally responsive, we don't mean that all their behavior is restricted to that segment of the continuum. Most of their behavior, though, occurs within a rather narrow band of the continuum.

It's often believed that people who are emotionally controlled simply lack feelings. However, above-the-line people may experience strong feelings. They're just less likely to display them.

Take Joe DiMaggio. Interviewer Warner Wolf said to him, "Joe, you had a reputation for being an unemotional player, as though you never felt the pressure. . . ."

"That's not true," DiMaggio responded. "They said I had a poker face, but I knew what was going on inside. All those years, my stomach was churning. Outside, I didn't show emotion. But inside I was plenty emotional."[1]

It's important to emphasize that for our purposes responsiveness refers to a person's *behavior*. It's about actions that anyone can see or hear—not about what is or is not going on inside the person. To help you picture what more responsive and less responsive behavior looks like, let's look at the profile of a "typical" person on each half of the responsiveness continuum.

Characteristic Behaviors of More Responsive People

Here's the sort of behavior you'll see and hear when you are with a more responsive person. Compared to the less responsive half of the population, the more responsive person tends to:

- Express feelings more openly
- Appear more friendly
- Be more facially expressive
- Gesture more freely
- Have more vocal inflection
- Be comfortable with small talk
- Use more anecdotes and stories
- Express more concern about the human aspect of issues
- Prefer working with people
- Dress more casually
- Be less structured in their use of time

More responsive people have most, but not necessarily all, of these characteristics.

Characteristic Behaviors of Less Responsive People

Less responsive people share most of the following behavioral characteristics. Compared to more responsive people, they tend to:

• Be less disclosing of feelings
• Appear more reserved
• Have less facial expressiveness
• Gesture less often
• Have less vocal inflection
• Be less interested in and less adept at "small talk"
• Use more facts and logic than anecdotes
• Be more task-oriented
• Prefer working alone
• Dress more formally
• Be more structured in their use of time

People who are less responsive than half the population have most but not necessarily all of these characteristics.

Wherever You Are on Each Axis, It's a Good Place to Be

Dr. Merrill, whose research highlighted the importance of assertiveness and responsiveness, conducted several studies to determine how each dimension of behavior is linked to a person's success. He and his colleague Roger Reid report:

> When our research was completed . . . we had evidence to challenge the notion that the most successful persons in business are more assertive. In addition, responsiveness or lack of it did not appear to be consistently related to success. Successful, well-regarded career persons were found along all ranges of the assertiveness and responsiveness scales—just as were less successful individuals.[2]

It's fortunate that people can be successful from any location on the assertiveness and responsiveness axes because it's virtually impossible to permanently change your characteristic level of either type of behavior.

Habit patterns related to these two crucial dimensions of behavior are deeply ingrained by the time we reach adulthood. For example, although it's possible to increase or decrease one's emotional expression at times, it is extremely difficult to fundamentally change one's characteristic degree of expression of emotion. Paul Eckman, a scholar noted for his studies on body language, writes: "Once any habit becomes established, operating automatically, not requiring awareness, it is hard to undo. I believe that those habits involving the management of emotion . . . may be the most difficult of all to break."[3]

People are often self-critical and want to change who they fundamentally are. Although self-development is a desirable activity, it's equally important to respect and even celebrate the fundamental and essentially unchangeable aspects of yourself. This includes accepting your characteristic degrees of assertiveness and responsiveness.

Assertiveness and responsiveness are two of the most important dimensions in a person's behavior. Taken together, these two patterns determine one's style.

Want to know your own style? We didn't point it out at the time, but it is your levels of assertiveness and responsiveness that you assessed on the Behavioral Inventory in Chapter Three. Now that you understand more about these two dimensions of behavior, you can see in Chapter Five how to use that information in calculating your style.

Chapter Five

Seeing Yourself as Others See You

As we've said, your style is determined by how *other people* perceive your behavior. It's always a challenge to get inside another person's frame of reference. It's especially difficult to objectively understand how others see you. Because it's so important and so challenging to see ourselves as others see us, in this chapter we describe several approaches you can take to ascertain your style.

Style Names: A Necessary Evil

To communicate easily about styles, each style must have a name. One of the problems in naming the styles is that people may focus only on what the label suggests to them rather than on the full spectrum of behaviors characteristic of that style. For example, the label "Driver," which is used to designate one of the styles, suggests only a part of that style's richness of behavior. By focusing on the label "Driver," some may think of such a person as autocratic, dictatorial, pushing people till they drop. Some Drivers are that way, but many are not. Like any other style, Drivers can be participative and empowering. Essentially, each style is far richer than what its label implies.

In Chapter Six, we provide a thorough description of each style. For the present, realize that *each style name is an indication of typical levels of assertiveness and responsiveness.*

Analyticals: Less assertive than half the population and less responsive (less emotionally disclosing) than half the population

Drivers: More assertive than half the population and less responsive (less emotionally disclosing) than half the population

24

Expressives: More assertive than half the population and more responsive (more emotionally disclosing) than half the population

Amiables: Less assertive than half the population and more responsive (more emotionally disclosing) than half the population

Which of the Four Styles Is Yours?

The Behavioral Inventory you filled out in Chapter Three is not a test. You can't pass or fail it; there is no better or worse combination of scores. Each style, as you'll recall, is a good place to be. Each style has tendencies to important strengths, and each has tendencies to some liabilities as well.

To ascertain your style, turn back to the Behavioral Inventory in Chapter Three. Count the number of boxes you checked in each column and record the total.

Here's what the numbers mean. The column farthest to the left is where you tallied the *left*-of-the-line (less assertive) behaviors that characterize you. The column next to it is where you tallied behaviors that are *right*-of-the-line (more assertive). Check the box below that represents the *higher* of these two scores:

❑ *left*-of-the-line ❑ *right*-of-the-line

The column farthest to the right is where you tallied the *below*-the-line (more emotionally responsive) behaviors that characterize you. The column just to the left of it stands for *above*-the-line (less emotionally responsive, more reserved) behaviors. Check the box below that represents the higher of these two scores:

❑ *above*-the-line ❑ *below*-the-line

If your highest scores are:

Left and above: You think others see you as an Analytical.
Right and above: You think others see you as a Driver.
Left and below: You think others see you as an Amiable.
Right and below: You think others see you as an Expressive.

In Figure 5–1, you can locate your assessment of your position on the styles grid.

Figure 5–1. A styles grid for self-assessment.

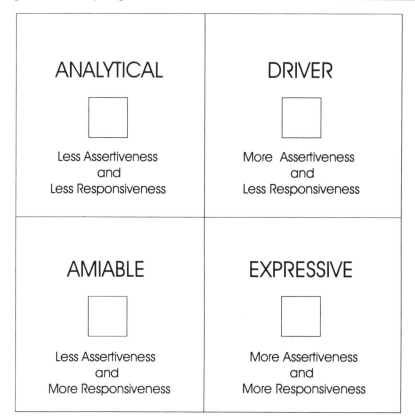

Further Assessments

As you consider what you read in Chapter Four, do you think most *other people* perceive you as more assertive or less assertive than half the population? More responsive or less responsive? This information helps place you in one of the quadrants of the grid. As you read further, you'll gain more information about behavioral styles that can help you assess how you come across to other people.

Another way to identify your style is to have three to five people who know you well use the Behavioral Inventory in Chapter Three with reference to your behaviors. This is a *guided* assessment since the lists direct people to base their assessment on specific behavioral criteria.

Now combine each person's feedback about whether he or she sees you as more or less assertive and more or less responsive than half the population. Using Figure 5–1, put a mark in the quadrant where the first person's feedback would place you. Do this with the feedback you received from each of the other people. You'll probably find that there's general but perhaps not total agreement about your style. It doesn't have to be unanimous. What you are looking for is an average portrait of how other people view your conduct.

Use Two or More Approaches

The image we have of ourselves is often based on how we *wish* to behave or how we *fear* we behave or how we would *like other people to see us*. These subjective hopes and fears distort our image of ourselves. As Ben Franklin put it in *Poor Richard's Almanac*, "There are three things extremely hard: steel, a diamond, and to know one's self." Although our research suggests that a person normally has about a 50 percent likelihood of assessing his or her own style correctly, that percentage can be improved considerably by combining several self-assessments, as suggested in this chapter. And your self-awareness can be further enhanced by obtaining feedback on your behavioral style from several people who know you well.

It's a valuable exercise to try to figure out your own style. *If you see yourself differently than other people see you, that's an important discrepancy to be aware of.* That's why we recommend that you do a self-assessment *and* receive input on your style based on the impressions of others. Since behavioral style is *how you are perceived by others,* it's crucial to get their feedback.

Want to know more about what makes you, and your co-workers, customers, and suppliers tick? Chapter Six describes the four styles.

Chapter Six

Four Paths to Success

You have a dominant style. In other words, you prefer to relate and work in ways characteristic of one of the four styles. Early in life, one style emerged as your favorite, and you now rely most on that style. Because it's become habitual, it's easiest for you to function that way. It's how you prefer to work most of the time: This is your "comfort zone."

Each style has potential *strengths and weaknesses*. The strengths are merely *potential* assets. These tendencies need to be cultivated in order to become actual strengths. Similarly, the weaknesses are merely *potential* liabilities. Successful persons of each style create ways to prevent these characteristics from undermining their effectiveness.

Although you have a dominant style, it's also true that *you are a four-style person*. Despite the fact that one style predominates in each person, behaviorally we're all a bit of a mixed bag. No one operates solely from one style. There's no such thing as an absolute Analytical. However strong our primary style may be, we can all find traces or even large doses of the other styles in our behavior. Like a right-handed person who learns to use the left hand, each person uses some behaviors associated with the other styles. To a degree, you and each of the people you meet are four-style people. You'll probably see parts of yourself in the description of each style.

Remember:

• *You can't change your dominant style.* You'll be that style for the rest of your life. You'll change in many other ways. But your dominant style is a fundamental part of who you are and will persist through your lifetime. Fortunately, as we've said repeatedly, no style is better than any other. They're all good places to be.

• *You are far more than your style.* Your style is a significant part of who you are—but it's only a part of you. Your personality includes your style—but there's much more to you than that. You are also the beliefs you hold dear, the values you're committed to, the goals you strive for, the relationships that nurture you, the idiosyncrasies that characterize you, and much more. Obviously, understanding another person's style doesn't tell us all there is to know about that person. Never forget that every person you meet is far more than his or her style.

• *You are different from others of your style.* People of a given style are similar to each other in important ways, but they are far from identical to one another. Like leaves on an oak tree, people of a given style are dissimilar in their similarity. Once you begin thinking of individuals within a particular style, the differences between them are striking. Think, for example, of some well-known Expressives: Muhammad Ali, Carol Burnett, Bill Clinton, Bill Cosby, Lee Iacocca, Jesse Jackson, Bobby Knight, Liza Minelli, Oprah Winfrey. They are all Expressives with important behavioral characteristics in common. Yet they're different in so many ways that it's hard to believe they could all be crammed into any one category.

One of the greatest traps that people fall into when contemplating PeopleStyles is ignoring the enormous individual differences that exist within each style. Don't allow yourself to fall into the simplistic mind-set that thinks, "If you've seen one, you've seen 'em all."

• *Your acceptance of each of the styles enables you to make this model work for you rather than against you.* Acceptance means recognition of a style's worth without implying approval of its limitations. With the mind-set of acceptance, you can celebrate the fundamental worth of each style. You can give balanced attention to strengths and weaknesses. As an accepting person who notes the downside of a person's style, you don't ignore or condone the behavior, but neither do you blow it out of proportion.

The opposite of acceptance is a judgmental mind-set. Anthropologist Margaret Mead noted that people tend to move quickly from awareness of diversity to concepts of superiority or inferiority. It's difficult to think of human differences without thinking in terms of better or worse. Unless they work at being objective, people are tempted to focus on the least desirable characteristics of other styles. They let the worst rather than the best exemplars color their impression of another style. They look at differences from their own style-based frame of reference and see the differences as flaws. Consequently, they are likely to disparage, put down, belittle, name-call, and poke fun at other styles. Not a great way to build relationships.

With effort, however, each of us can learn to view other styles with acceptance and even appreciation. We can realize how boring life would be if we were all of the same style. Variety is indubitably the spice of life. We can be grateful that other people enjoy doing some of the things that we dislike doing and that we aren't particularly good at. When you accept the other styles and celebrate their strengths, you are able to build productive relationships with people very different from yourself. So as you read these descriptions of the four styles, make a conscious effort to approach each with appreciation.

• *It takes all styles to make an effective organization.* Each style has important strengths but lacks the strengths of other styles. Effective organizations require the strengths of all four styles. Peter Drucker, the organizational analyst, wrote, "The top-management tasks require at least four different kinds of human beings: the 'thought man' [Analytical], the 'action man' [Driver], the 'people man' [Amiable], and the 'front man' [Expressive]."[1]

Analyticals

The style in the upper-left portion of the grid is called Analytical. People in this quadrant combine considerable emotional restraint with less than average assertiveness (see Figure 6–1).

The Analytical is the most perfectionistic of the styles. Analytical

Figure 6–1. Analyticals show less-than-average responsiveness and less-than-average assertiveness.

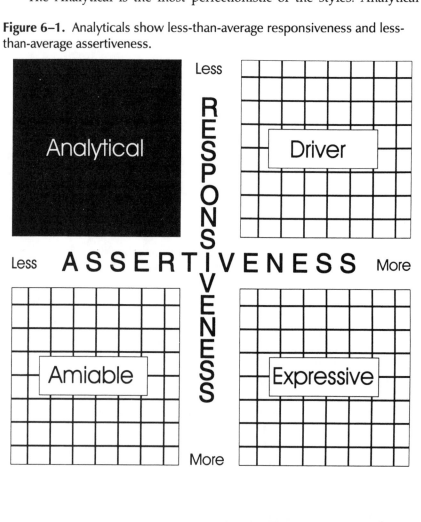

people want things they're associated with to be *right*. Some styles shoot from the hip. "Ready, fire, aim," advises one well-known management consultant, but Analyticals are appalled at such advice. Long before the current quality movement, they were urging, "Let's do it right so we won't have to do it over." They set very high standards and are willing to do the time-consuming work needed to achieve or exceed those standards. Analyticals are sticklers for detail, since they believe that vigorous attention to every aspect of a project, no matter how insignificant, contributes to the final outcome.

Analyticals tend to be the most critical of the styles. Because of their perfectionistic tendencies, they are often very hard on themselves—and on others. Their exacting standards cause them to be generally very sparing with compliments and expressions of appreciation. Analyticals need to guard against these tendencies, because it can be demoralizing to work for someone who is big on criticism and small on compliments.

The Analytical is known for being systematic and well-organized. At best, this style is adept at building highly effective processes that produce consistently outstanding results. At its worst, however, the Analytical's methodical bent can degenerate into the bureaucracy of excessive regulations and a by-the-book mentality.

This style craves data. The more, the better. When you see an effective Analytical converting that data into useful information, you understand the truth of the old saying, "knowledge is power."

When facing risks, the Analytical tends to be prudent. Many take calculated risks, but some are reluctant to do even that. As a rule, they'd rather be safe than sorry.

Don't expect these prudent people to be cavalier about decision making. They want to be *certain* of making the right choice. But such certainty is not possible. Analyticals gather as much information as they can; even so, there's seldom enough data about the options for them to be comfortable about making a decision. They try to weigh the options, which usually include imponderables. As a result, Analyticals often agonize over decisions. Some become stressed about even small decisions such as what to order when eating out.

An Analytical likes to be alone or with just a few other people. If possible, she leaves the big gatherings and cocktail parties to others; she'd rather stay home and read a book. A person of this style is rarely linked closely to the grapevine but may be tapped into the Internet. An Analytical who has an office can usually be found in it . . . and the door is probably closed. An Analytical has to be pushed to manage by walking around. In fact, she typically prefers working alone to working with others. Despite the Analytical's solitary nature, she surprises you by being loyal when the going gets rough. Though this style isn't overtly people-ori-

ented, in crunch situations the Analytical often tries to see that employees
are treated fairly.

The Analytical's body language is low-key. They walk more slowly
than right-of-the-line folks. They tend to lean back in their chair even
when making a point. Analyticals don't gesture much, and their gestures
tend to be smaller, less flowing, and less emphatic than is common. Nor
are they noted for having much eye contact or facial expressiveness. They
tend to dress conservatively. If they have an office, they probably prefer
businesslike decor.

The Analytical is the quietest of the styles. They tend to speak less
often than people of other styles—except when delving into great detail
on a topic. When the Analytical talks, the volume is low, the pace is slow,
and there's little inflection in the voice. People of this style like to think
things through before speaking. They continue thinking as they talk,
scanning their minds for the right word or phrase to communicate content accurately. This leads to frequent hesitations, which others may find
annoying. Also, since they are thinking about what they say as they
speak, they're apt to interrupt themselves in midsentence and begin a
new thought that just came to mind—a trait that often confuses listeners.
It's easy to see why a person of this style tends to favor written over
spoken communication.

The content of an Analytical's conversation has some distinguishing
characteristics. When talking, an Analytical typically is more task-oriented than people-oriented. He approaches issues logically and, even in
casual conversation, is apt to break what he's saying into points: "In the
first place . . . ," "Secondly . . . ," and so forth. Analyticals strive for
accuracy and expect it in others. They want people to furnish them with
details; when they explain something, they normally give more minutiae
than people of other styles want. They're more apt to analyze an issue
and see the complexity involved than they are to decisively recommend
a course of action. Harry Truman, one of our more assertive presidents,
used to say he wanted a one-armed economist; he was tired of advisers
who said, "On the one hand this, but on the other hand that." The right-
of-the-line Truman undoubtedly said that after a conference with Analyticals, who are adept at elaborating on the intricacies of a problem but
won't make a clear-cut recommendation.

Analyticals tend to be indirect when making a request or stating an
opinion. The comment "Perhaps we should consider such and so" may
mean "I think we should do it." Sometimes an Analytical asks a question
but is really making a statement. "Do you think it would be wise to . . . ?"
may mean "I'd like you to take this action."

Analyticals don't wear feelings on their sleeve. They may feel as
deeply about an issue as anyone else, but they'll probably talk about the
facts of the case rather than their feelings about it. They often intellectual-

ize feelings, both their own and those of other people. People often find Analyticals hard to read because they show so little emotion. Sometimes Analyticals are not in touch with their own feelings. Their heads shout so loudly that they can't hear what their guts are saying.

The Analytical tries to avoid the emotionality that's related to conflict. When others get carried away by emotion, Analyticals retreat into their heads and become emotionally detached. People of this style assume a rational approach will cool an overheated situation. It often has the opposite result. Expressives, in particular, become even more upset when an Analytical tries to get them to talk calmly and rationally during a conflict. When the Analytical avoids conflict, important issues are tabled, problems are left unattended, and significant opportunities may be missed.

When it comes to time management, the Analytical is a strange mix. She tends to be punctual for appointments but tardy in meeting deadlines. It's easy to see why this style would tend to miss deadlines. Analyticals' perfectionistic quest for quality leads them to set exceedingly high standards. At the same time, they do things more slowly and deliberately than most people. They examine more options. They research each alternative with exceptional thoroughness. When the research is finally concluded, they take an unusually long time to arrive at a decision. Every aspect of the Analytical's pacing is slower than that of the more assertive styles.

No one is completely true to type. The average Analytical will have most of the characteristics described above but not all of them. So when working with an Analytical, be alert to the characteristics of this style but also look for behaviors that may be exceptions to the rule.

As with each of the styles, there are pluses and minuses to the Analytical's way of doing things. When people do this style poorly, it's not a productive way of working. However, Analyticals who use their style well are on a great pathway to success.

Since 25 percent of the population are Analyticals, you are likely dealing with these folks every day. In Part Two of this book and in the four Appendixes, we show you how to develop stronger work relationships with these quiet and industrious people.

Amiables

Another type of person you're working with is the Amiable. This style is located in the lower-left quadrant (see Figure 6–2). The Amiable gets things done in a manner that's less assertive than average, combined with more-than-average responsiveness.

As you can see from Figure 6–2, the Amiable and the Analytical

Figure 6–2. Amiables show more-than-average responsiveness and less-than-average assertiveness.

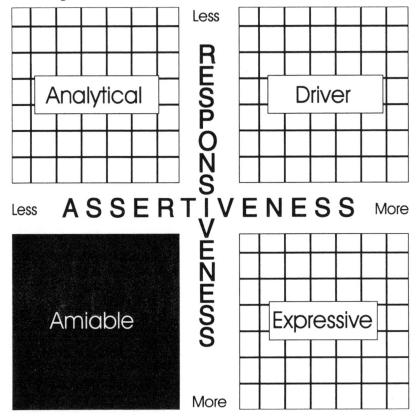

share a similar level of assertiveness. Therefore, in this portrait, you find numerous similarities between Amiables and Analyticals. The difference between these two left-of-the-line styles is in their degree of responsiveness. The Amiable shows considerably more emotion than the Analytical, and this distinction is connected to a number of other behavioral differences between the two styles.

To a greater degree than is typical of other styles, the Amiable is a team player. He normally prefers working with others, especially in small groups or one-on-one. He doesn't seek the spotlight and seldom gets into ego clashes with others. Amiables are less likely than the more assertive styles to seek power for themselves. They can be skilled at encouraging others to expand on their ideas and are good at seeing value in other people's contributions. As a result of their openness to the opinions of others, they are sometimes able to salvage a person's worthwhile ideas that other team members are quick to discount. People of this style may also be adept at integrating conflicting opinions into a synthesis that all parties can genuinely support.

Amiables' effectiveness as team players is enhanced by their generosity with their time. If a co-worker asks for advice or help, they drop what they're doing to help. They often volunteer to do unglamorous, out-of-the-limelight activities for the team. Because of their dedicated backstage work, they are the unsung heroes of many a team effort. While this unselfishness is often constructive, the Amiable may overdo it to such an extent as to default on delivering his or her own commitments in a timely manner.

The Amiable's quiet friendliness is an asset in working with people. Both below-the-line styles, the Amiables and the Expressives, are very people-oriented. The Expressive, though, is more rambunctious about it. The Amiable takes more of a low-key approach. With an easygoing, likable manner, the Amiable appears to build relationships more easily than most people. Ties to others are often more personal than is characteristic of the other styles.

People of this style back up their friendliness with empathy. They're generally more interested in hearing your concerns than they are in expressing their own. Amiables are especially sensitive to other people's feelings. When compassion is appropriate, it shows on their faces and in their eyes as well as in their words. Consequently, people tend to confide in them.

The Amiable usually performs best in a stable, clearly structured situation. This style is not as enamored of goal setting and planning as the above-the-line types. Amiables often prefer to have the organization define their role and set their goals—as long as the demands aren't unreasonable. Once their role is clarified and the direction is set, they work steadily in the performance of their duties. As a rule, people of this style are industrious, service-oriented workers. Because of their easygoing, friendly, unpretentious ways, other people may not realize how much work they turn out.

Some Amiables, however, overdo their friendliness and are sidetracked from task by their desire to relate to people. If all work can be said to consist of task aspects and people aspects, Drivers and Analyticals are prone to overemphasize the task while Amiables and Expressives may give disproportionate time and attention to their relationships with people.

Some people are better at creating products, organizations, etc., while others are better at maintaining them. Amiables shine as maintainers. They value what has already been created and find satisfaction in working to preserve it. Also, to a greater degree than most people, Amiables are comfortable doing routine procedures and following processes established by others.

The Amiable, like the Analytical, tends to be indecisive and takes a cautious approach to decision making, looking for guarantees to lower the risks involved. This style touches base with the people affected by a decision before coming to a final conclusion. Amiables often delay making decisions, especially when risk is involved or when it's a controversial call and people are likely to be upset by the outcome. However, Amiables may also delay making a decision simply because they find it so uncomfortable to make a clear-cut choice.

The Amiable is conscientious, but not enthusiastic, about reading memos and reports, preferring instead to hear directly from people. So when they can, Amiables talk face-to-face or get on the phone. Many are well connected to the grapevine.

Amiables are patient with other people and with organizations. They may gripe about a bad situation, but they're likely to carry on. They do have a limit, though. If you persist too long in treating them in ways they don't like, they'll eventually become angry and will be very slow to forgive or forget.

The Amiable's body language is low-key. This style walks more slowly than more-assertive styles and has less erect posture. They often lean back in their chair even when making a request or stating an opinion. Amiables rely on gestures when communicating; and their movement tends to be fluid and graceful, though not dramatic. They're comfortable with eye contact and are facially expressive. In conversation, Amiables tend to use less "air time" than the more assertive styles. They're usually slower in forming an opinion about a recommended course of action than Drivers or Expressives. So when a course of action is being discussed, the Amiable's input tends to come late in the session or not at all. The Amiable's voice is warm and the volume is low. This style also speaks more slowly than right-of-the-line styles. Their taste in clothes can be characterized as appropriate and, when the situation allows, casual. (Of course, people of any style may be influenced by dress-for-success literature or may wear clothing that others pick out for them.)

The Amiable's conversation is more people-oriented than task-oriented. People of this style are gracious with small talk. They speak more about people and feelings than the above-the-line styles. They're apt to ask you how your trip went last week or how your child did in a recent game or competition. Their focus on people and feelings continues when the discussion turns to work issues. Few, if any, topics are strictly business for people of this style. They wonder, for example, how people in the department feel about the new procedure being discussed. This consistent attention to the human component of work can enhance morale and make the process of change far less disruptive than it might be without the Amiable's influence.

It's often thought that Amiables are very disclosing. Their facial expressions seem very open. In conversation, Amiables reveal personal things about themselves that make people feel they know them better than they know most people. Often, however, Amiables are surprisingly guarded. They don't communicate many of the thoughts and feelings that are important to them. This type of person especially withholds feelings of anger and critical judgments of others. The Amiable can seem calm on the outside while a storm rages within.

When Amiables make a request or state an opinion, they're inclined to phrase it indirectly. They often state their point of view by asking a question. Rather than declaring, "Let's move ahead with Campaign X," she might ask, "Do you think Campaign X is the way to go?" Or she may quote others who share the same opinion: "A lot of people are saying that Campaign X is the way to go." The asking-oriented tendency of the Amiable may become too pronounced, leading people to complain, "I don't know where Peter is coming from. I wish he'd take a clear stand on things."

When people work together, there's bound to be conflict. Some conflict is productive, although much is destructive. Because Amiables treasure harmonious relationships, they are natural peacemakers and are often found pouring oil on troubled water. Their efforts at conciliation often make continued collaboration possible. At times, though, they go overboard in their efforts and try to smooth things over even when hard issues must be faced and resolved.

Many Amiables are reluctant to tell it like it is for fear of alienating the other person. When opinions are divided about a course of action, Amiables are more likely than the average person to withhold their point of view. They may hesitate to contest a point, even when they think they're right and important issues are at stake. They may dislike conflict so much that they say what they think the other person wants to hear rather than what they really believe. Amiables who don't overcome this reticence to take a stand lose credibility with people who doubt they can count on them when the chips are down.

Another drawback related to the Amiable's need to maintain pleasant relationships is an unwillingness to confront a person's performance problems. Amiables tend to avoid giving corrective feedback. Yet they may be more critical than they let on. They may voice to a third party the critique that would do more good if stated directly to the person being criticized. As a manager, the Amiable can be slow to a fault in dealing with an employee's inadequate performance. This style is often squeamish about using authority, and when they finally apply it, they may use it inconsistently.

High-performing Amiables overcome the tendency to conceal true opinions. Yet they preserve their concern for the other person and the desire not to harm the relationship. Their tact enables them to say hard things while leaving the other person's ego intact. Their diplomatic timing and phrasing may enable their message to get through to people who were closed to the same idea expressed more bluntly by others.

When we give a general description of a style, we're speaking of broad tendencies. Few Amiables have all the characteristics we've described. People of other styles have some characteristics typical of Amiables. As we've said, this is especially true of Analyticals, who share their lower degree of assertiveness. Expressives also share some characteristics with Amiables because both styles have more responsiveness than average. Although a given Amiable may not have all the tendencies described in this section and although people of other styles may have some of these tendencies, this portrait distinguishes Amiables from each of the other styles.

Since 25 percent of the population are Amiables, you'll be spending a lot of time with these folks. As with each of the other styles, there are potential strengths and weaknesses associated with the Amiable style. And, like the other styles, Amiables who work their style effectively are on a sound pathway to success.

Expressives

You also find a lot of Expressives in the workplace. This style is located in the lower-right portion of the grid (see Figure 6–3). People in this quadrant integrate a high level of assertiveness with much emotional expression (responsiveness).

We've already mentioned that Amiables and Expressives have some characteristics in common because both styles show more responsiveness than most people. Later in the chapter, you'll note similarities between Expressives and Drivers because the two styles are highly assertive. There are a number of characteristics, however, that are distinctive to the Expressive.

This is the most flamboyant of the styles. Expressives tend toward the dramatic. They like bright colors, bold statements, and eye-catching projects. This style thrives on being in the limelight and seems to gravitate naturally to center stage.

This spirited style bristles with energy. The Expressive seems to have pep enough for any two people. Expressives' vim, vigor, and vitality are evident in nearly everything they do. The sheer energy of Expressives, when combined with other aspects of their high assertiveness, can make them seem overwhelming at times. Every once in a while, a person of this style temporarily runs out of steam, but that usually takes place when the stimulus of other people is missing. Because their sluggish moments

Figure 6–3. Expressives show more-than-average assertiveness and more-than-average responsiveness.

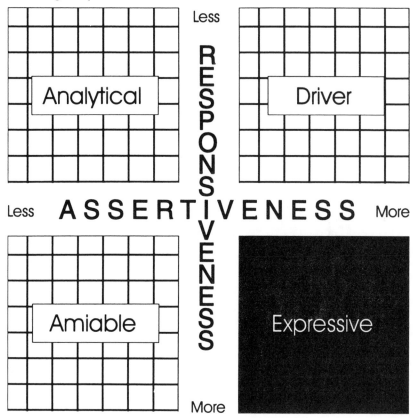

occur when no one is around, the Expressive seems even more tirelessly energetic than is actually the case.

Perhaps because of their abundant energy, Expressives want to be continually on the go. They don't like to spend too long in any one spot, and they enjoy being where the action is. So you often see them walking about or hopping into the car. They hate to be confined to a desk all day long. I phone an Expressive and the secretary tells me, "He's away from his desk right now." I chuckle. He's always away from his desk.

When required to sit through a long meeting, an Expressive's restless energy is still evident. She continuously shifts about in her chair. She's always moving her feet or legs, gesturing with her hands and arms, toying with a paper clip or pencil, or drumming her fingers on the table. When bored at meetings, the Expressive is unlikely to be subtly tuned out; rather, she'll be engaged in a side conversation—or fully, obviously, intensely, and unmistakably disengaged.

The Expressive is the most outgoing of the styles. In contrast to the Amiable who conveys quiet friendliness, the Expressive takes a more hale-and-hearty approach to people. This style is interpersonally proactive. Despite some inner qualms that may rise at times, these people seem to relate easily and effortlessly to strangers. As a result, a person of this outgoing style tends to have a larger circle of acquaintances than do people of other styles.

When Expressives have a choice of doing something alone or with other people, they prefer to link up with others. They invite people for lunch, to play tennis after work, or to go cycling on the weekend. When they travel out of town, they make the effort to look up old acquaintances in the area they're visiting. This high-contact type of person spends considerable time on the telephone with lots of people. The Expressive is well tapped into the grapevine. As you'd imagine, this style prefers work that requires much interaction with people. These people, who are such naturals at networking, have innumerable contacts who can help them achieve their goals. People of this style lend credibility to the saying, "Who you know is as important as what you know."

Expressives tend to be dreamers. Their vision is typically bold and imaginative. They push people to look beyond the merely mundane and practical. They love blue-skying sessions, where imagination can soar without concern for pragmatic constraints. Every organization needs people who can envision great projects and who can conceive a bigger, better, and brighter future for the department or organization. Expressives help co-workers rise above a prosaic and unimaginative approach to work.

It's been said that to create castles in the air, it's necessary to build the foundations under them. That's where many Expressives are weak. They resist getting sufficiently involved in the nitty-gritty, even when it is essential to achieving their dream. This style likes to focus more on broad generalizations than on specific facts. The Expressive is interested in the forest rather than the trees and is content to have others do the details. When you and others are hard at work with the nitty-gritty effort to build the foundation under a castle in the air that an Expressive sold you on, you may find that he is not working along with you. He's off dreaming of other castles rather than helping to finish the one at hand.

Expressives are impulsive. They have a tendency to act first and think later. Many Expressives use a particular image to describe this aspect of their style: "First I dive into the pool, and then I look to see if there's any water in it." As a result of this tendency, people of this style have to work their way out of more than their share of problems which are of their own making. After observing an Expressive friend trying to recover from yet another crisis that seemed unnecessary, an Analytical tactfully asked why she didn't plan ahead to avoid the needless hassles. "Ultimately," said the Expressive, "*my* way takes *less* time. You Analyticals plan for eventualities that never happen. And planning is such a drag. Besides, I like the excitement of improvising myself out of these jams. It's a lot better than all that planning."

The impulsiveness of Expressives often creates problems for themselves and others in the workplace. They prefer to work according to opportunity rather than according to plan. Few are good at time management. These easily diverted people pay less attention to clock time and calendar time than other styles do. They're often late to meetings or may miss them altogether. And they're often behind schedule with projects. Some habitually miss deadlines. Others become adept at catching up at the last minute. People are likely to get annoyed at the Expressive's seemingly free and easy approach to time.

The Expressive's own feelings have a powerful impact on him. More than any other style, he's on an emotional roller coaster. When emotionally high, he's ecstatic; when low, he tends to be in the pits. People often find it difficult to deal with these emotional extremes. Yet, because of their emotionality, the Expressives' enthusiasm in "up" times is contagious. Though people of each style can be good motivators, the Expressive is often exceptionally effective at helping people recharge their emotional batteries.

Expressives are playful and fun-loving. They usually find a way to schedule some recreation into a crowded day. These people love a good time themselves, and they enjoy prompting happiness in others. They like to tell jokes, describe humorous incidents, think up pranks, and laugh heartily. A person noted for throwing great parties said that one key to a lively gathering is to make sure there are a number of Expressives in the group.

Expressives look for ways to make work more enjoyable—maybe even fun. They're apt to suggest you meet in the coffee shop rather than at the office. They may kid around for a few minutes before plunging into the topic at hand. They'll often find a humorous slant on something in an otherwise serious discussion. One Expressive CEO we know gave each new employee a Mickey Mouse wristwatch. "If work ever stops being fun," he'd say, "turn in your watch and find a job you enjoy." This very competitive CEO assumed that if you have fun at work, not only is it better for you but you'll be more productive, too.

When Expressives talk, their whole body joins in. Like the Amiables, they use flowing gestures—but they use more of them, and the motions are bigger and more forceful. Their facial expressions are the most communicative of all the styles. More than any other style, Expressives modulate the pitch and tone of voice to match what they are saying. The constantly changing inflection helps to hold people's attention. With their entire body language helping to communicate their message, Expressives at their best can do an exceptional job of getting a point across to an individual, a group, or a large audience.

Expressives are definitely *tell*-assertive. They advocate more than they inquire. They're more into talking than listening. They have a tendency to interrupt others and monopolize the conversation. Though Expressives may be perceptive in what they say and entertaining in the way they say it, they sometimes turn people off by their one-sided conversations.

The hale and hearty Expressive speaks with a loud voice. In a restaurant, it may be easier to hear the Expressive four tables away than it is to hear your left-of-the-line dinner partner sitting directly across from you.

Expressives are the most verbally fluent of the styles. Their words seem to flow effortlessly. They appear to have a large vocabulary, with immediate access to it. People of this style tend to speak very rapidly. Only a few Drivers can match their speaking pace.

When Expressives talk, they often "think out loud." As an Expressive friend put it, "I speak to find out what I'm thinking." Digressions are par for the course for this style. When an Expressive is holding the floor, she may skip from topic to topic in ways that seem to defy logic.

Storytelling is part and parcel of the Expressive's way of communicating. He breaks the ice with a joke or a humorous incident that happened to him or to a mutual acquaintance. When making a point, he's more likely to cite an example than to present a string of facts. He probably won't quote any statistics—unless, of course, the numbers are very dramatic.

Regarding the content of their conversations, Expressives are more people-oriented than task-oriented. It's not that they're disinterested in getting the task done; it's just that their manner of doing it has more of a people focus. For example, if you meet with an Expressive about a specific issue, don't expect to get to the point right away. If the Expressive takes the lead, as will undoubtedly happen, the initial part of the conversation is likely to be about both of you and other people, and she may tell a story or two before focusing on the issue. For the Expressive, these topics aren't beside the point but are an important prelude to conversations about substantive issues. Above-the-line styles who are more task-focused often consider that this extended rapport building is a waste of time and may get tense waiting for the Expressive to get to business. The Expressive thinks this is business: "After all, what is business if it's not people talking to each other?"

The Expressive is apt to be up-front about saying what he does or doesn't like about your proposal or your behavior. This is a tell-it-like-it-is style. Although Expressives may mean no offense, their comments sometimes seem abrasive, especially to less assertive folks. Yet this willingness to raise the hard issues, which can be crucial to productivity, may stimulate people to work on issues that require attention.

Not every Expressive, of course, has all these characteristics. And, depending on their degree of assertiveness and responsiveness, their behaviors may be more muted or exaggerated than described here. Still, you surely recognize your Expressive colleagues and friends already in this description.

Since 25 percent of the population are Expressives, you spend a lot of time with these highly assertive and highly responsive folks. As with the other styles, this one has its potential strengths and weaknesses. When Expressives do their style effectively, they can be very productive and effective.

Drivers

The other type of person you work with is the Driver. This style is located in the upper right area of the grid (see Figure 6–4). Drivers blend a higher-than-average level of assertiveness with less-than-average responsiveness.

The Driver is very results-focused. This, the most practical of the styles, prides itself on its bottom-line orientation. A strong goal orientation characterizes the Driver. This style loves nothing more than to set high yet realistic objectives and then set about accomplishing them. However, these are very independent people; they want to set their own goals rather than have someone else set them.

The Driver is a get-it-done type of person. While an Analytical is thinking about a problem, an Amiable is meeting about it, and an Expressive is talking about it, the Driver is doing something about it. The action may not be the best solution, but the Driver feels relieved because something's getting done.

The Driver believes, with Thomas Carlyle, that "Our business is not to see what lies at a distance, but to do what lies clearly at hand." Unfortunately, with their excessive focus on the immediate situation, Drivers may not give sufficient consideration to the long-range implications of their actions.

Decisiveness is a salient characteristic of Drivers. They don't agonize over decisions as left-of-the-line styles do. The Analytical is seeking to make the right decision. The Amiable is looking for guarantees that the outcome will be satisfactory. The Driver takes a different approach to decision making. Drivers believe that indecision *is* a decision, and inevitably a bad one. Also, they're not compulsive about the quality of their decisions. "When you are 55 percent sure," they say, "it's time to act. If you wait until you are 95 percent sure, you won't succeed in this competi-

Figure 6–4. Drivers show more-than-average assertiveness and less-than-average responsiveness.

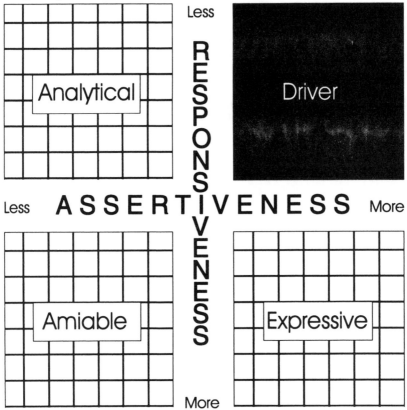

tive and very fast-paced environment." Rather than try to make the right decision each time, rather than secure guarantees that every decision will work out, the Driver says, "If six out of ten of my decisions pan out, I'm ahead of the game." When a decision turns out poorly, the Driver often takes it philosophically: "You win some, you lose some." This seemingly offhand approach to important decisions often seems irresponsible to left-of-the-line styles.

In matters of opinion and of policy, Drivers are more likely to change their mind than are the less assertive styles—Analyticals or Amiables. Because Drivers are so purposeful and rational, people are often surprised by the abrupt changes in their thinking and the sudden shifts in plans. It's not unlike a Driver to do an about-face that leaves everybody astounded. President Richard Nixon, a Driver, was one of Communism's implacable foes for years. Then he surprised the world by establishing diplomatic ties with Communist China.

Drivers are often puzzled by others' strong reactions to their reversals of position. The Analytical's tendency to theorize and to commit to principles creates a fairly consistent outlook. The Amiable is generally more wedded to the status quo than the Driver. The Amiable also anticipates the emotional discomfort people will experience as a result of the change. The Driver, however, is more focused on the immediate situation than on theory or principle or feelings. In the Driver's mind, the situation has changed and the response needs to change. And that appraisal may be accurate. However, Drivers are sometimes so fast-paced and action-oriented that they may improvise a hasty and ill-conceived course of action that merely sets the stage for a new batch of problems.

Drivers typically excel at time management. Books and courses on this topic usually consist of a smorgasbord of methods that are characterized by task orientation and efficiency. Once, when we studied the time management practices of three hundred managers, we found that the way the Drivers worked was by far the closest match to the usual cluster of time management methods.

The Driver's body language suggests purposefulness. Her posture is erect. She seems to lean into everything she does. She walks and moves faster than most people. Gestures, though fewer, smaller, and less flowing than the Expressive's, can be very forceful. The Driver's facial expression tends to be more serious than that of the below-the-line styles and more intense than that of the Analytical. When stating her point of view, the Driver's eye contact is direct—sometimes to the listener's discomfort.

Like every other characteristic, Drivers' speech is fast-paced. There's little vocal inflection. Drivers are quite forthright in stating their opinions or making requests. They're factual but not detailed, rational but not theoretical, direct and to the point. Combine this no-frills conversational style with rapid delivery, a leaning-in posture, forceful gestures, and eye contact that may seem piercing, and you can understand why some less assertive people can be intimidated by the Driver's style of communication.

A Driver takes a task-oriented approach to communication. He may discipline himself to engage in a little "small talk," but it's not his forte and the effort to build rapport may seem forced. Once the preliminaries are dispensed with, Drivers often rat-a-tat their way through the agenda until your time's up. The slower-paced Analytical and Amiable may feel bulldozed by this quick and relentless push through the agenda. The Amiable and the Expressive, whose behaviors are more people-oriented, are apt to reflect, "He didn't even treat us like *people*." Drivers can accomplish a tremendous amount in a short time. However, if people feel bulldozed or depersonalized, there's a danger that the progress may be more illusory than real. Other people's lack of buy-in or outright resistance may delay or even sabotage the outcome.

When we say the Driver is task-oriented rather than people-oriented, we don't imply a lack of caring about people. A Driver may have sincere concern for other people but just not talk about it as much as a below-the-line person might. Nor does this style's body language reveal the depth of concern they may have for others. Drivers are doers, and their feelings are often channeled into the language of action. Over the years, we've witnessed the trauma of downsizing in one corporation after another and have seen a number of Drivers make a greater effort to give concrete, tangible assistance to those affected than have many of their colleagues who appeared more concerned.

The Driver's high energy, fast pace, purposefulness, and directness of speech can trigger resentment in people. People often think of the Driver as being the most assertive of the styles. Yet the Expressive style is as assertive as the Driving style. The difference between the two styles, you recall, is that the Expressive is much more responsive—more emotionally disclosing and people-oriented. The Expressive is apt to inquire about your spouse and kids and tell you about a humorous incident that happened last week. Expressives fool around some of the time and entertain with stories, wisecracks, and jokes. Appearing as it does in this below-the-line package of behaviors, assertiveness may seem less stark than it otherwise would. By contrast, the Driver comes across as purposeful rather than playful. She's perceived as task-oriented rather than people-oriented. So when she's assertive, that's what you see—and typically little else. Consequently, a Driver may *seem* more forceful than an equally assertive Expressive.

Obviously, not all Drivers match this description in every detail. But by and large, this portrait should be a fairly good description of the Drivers you know.

Since 25 percent of the population are Drivers, you spend considerable time with these highly assertive, emotionally restrained folks. This style is neither better nor worse than the other styles. Just different. Drivers who use their style effectively can be very productive and effective.

Chapter Seven
Styles Under Stress

Sidney Waldheim, a sales manager, awakened with thoughts about the weekly sales meeting he'd be leading later in the day. "Sales are down for the quarter," he mused, "but everyone's trying hard. What's needed is a really 'up' meeting that will motivate everyone."

While he was dressing, it was impossible not to notice the glowering silence of his wife, Alicia. She was still angry about something he did yesterday, but she wouldn't discuss it. Sidney didn't even know what he'd done to upset her.

Sidney was steaming inside—Alicia's silent treatment nearly always got to him—but he decided not to make matters worse by blowing up. So he rushed to his car and barreled off to work. He tried to think about the upcoming sales meeting, but his mind kept careening back to Alicia's icy anger. His body tensed, and without thinking, he pressed harder on the accelerator. He heard a siren, saw flashing lights, and was motioned to the side of the road. The police officer told him he'd been doing 52 in a 35 mph zone. Sidney realized that this latest traffic violation would put him in the assigned-risk category; his car insurance costs would sky-rocket.

Sidney's head was throbbing when he got to the office. "What a way to start the day," he grumbled to himself. His phone rang. It was the regional sales manager, who was livid. The regional manager shouted into the phone that for the fourth month in a row Sidney's district had the lowest sales volume in the region. He told Sidney to turn things around quickly "or else."

Talk about stress! Sidney's glands pumped adrenaline into his al-ready-hyper system. His muscles were tense, his nerves were taut, and he had a headache. He popped two Advil and stalked into the sales meeting. Stress was directing his behavior. His carefully planned approach, which was to be motivational, was abandoned. Instead, he told his salespeople what a lousy job they were doing. He told them they were lazy. And he threatened, "If you don't sell more, we'll find people who will."

Back in his office, Sidney felt better. He'd gotten rid of much of his stress. Where did it go? It went to each of the salespeople in that meeting.

Sidney dumped his load of stress all over them, and now they had to cope with it on top of all the other stresses they were already handling. As you can imagine, no one left the meeting with a soaring motivation to sell. Instead, some were angry, some were hurt, some were worried. But not one was pumped up to go out and sell.

Sidney's relief from stress was only temporary, however. A major customer was furious about a late delivery. Although there was nothing Sidney could have done about it, the customer took his frustrations out on Sidney. That triggered the adrenaline overload all over again. When he arrived home after work, he was still steaming. He lit into one of his kids before heading into the den. He turned the TV on, but mainly he mentally replayed the disaster he'd made of his day. "They deserved it," he said to himself. But he knew his behavior had cost him. He shook his head and muttered aloud to himself, "I should have stayed in bed. I'd have been farther ahead."

Sidney, an Expressive, had moved into what is called *backup style* in response to an overload of stress. His reaction to excessive stress was predictable. So were the results: strained relationships, poor decisions, and lowered performance.

No style handles excess stress graciously. Each style has its own form of backup behavior. When people move into backup, their behavior has just one goal: to reduce their own stress. The trouble is, backup behavior usually generates stress in other people. It's not uncommon for a vicious circle to get started that can permanently mar relationships.

At times, each of us suffers an overload of stress which tends to bring out the worst in us. This chapter helps you understand backup styles, the changes in behavior that generally occur when people's stress gets out of hand. We talk about the link between each style and a particular backup style. As you'll see, backup behavior serves some protective functions, but it has a negative effect on decision making, productivity, and relationships. Finally, in this chapter you learn about preventive measures to lessen the amount of time you spend in backup. You also discover ways to limit the negative consequences when you are in backup and what to do when someone else is in backup. This understanding of backup styles helps you be more effective in dealing with exceptionally tense situations.

What Is a Backup Style?

People move from their normal style into a characteristic backup style in response to excessive stress. Unintentionally, their behavior becomes more extreme and inflexible.

Backup style is a response to *excessive levels of stress*. Some stress, of course, is desirable. Dr. Hans Selye, the father of stress research, found that stress adds spice to life. In the proper amounts, stress adds zest to our days and enhances our performance. That's why athletes try to get themselves psyched up for a competition.

Excessive stress, though, is uncomfortable, even dangerous. While backup behavior provides a way of relieving some of a person's own stress, it usually generates stress in others.

The switch from normal to backup behavior is not a conscious choice. It just pops out of people, automatically. In response to a stressful situation, a person's normal style-based behavior becomes *extreme*. The person pushes his regular tendencies to the hilt. Backup behavior is overkill.

- *Expressives*, who are usually socially engaging, *attack.*
- *Drivers*, who are normally directive, become *autocratic.*
- *Amiables*, who are typically supportive and cooperative, *acquiesce.*
- *Analyticals*, who are usually quiet and less emotional, *avoid* participation and emotional involvement.

Figure 7–1 shows that the backup behavior people typically move to is a more extreme manifestation of their normal style-based tendencies.

In backup, people's behavior becomes *inflexible*. They respond not to what the interpersonal situation calls for but to the stress they're feeling, regardless of the wishes or feelings of others. When in backup, people do things in an *extreme* way, letting the chips fall where they may. People in backup are *nonnegotiable* about their way of interacting with others. In response to stress, more than at any other time, people express "my way, not your way" behavior.

As we've noted, each style has its own way of handling excess stress. Here's a description of each of the four backup styles and of how people typically react to them.

Expressives in Backup: Attacking

Under normal circumstances Expressives are people-oriented. When overloaded with tension, they focus their frustrations on other people. These normally assertive and emotive people become even more assertive and emotionally unrestrained when they're stressed. In backup, they often resort to strong and abusive language, a loud, often shouting voice, and emphatic and belligerent gestures. Someone is usually the butt of the loud, exaggerated, angry personal attack by the Expressive who is in backup.

Ralph Waldo Emerson said, "We boil at different degrees." Expressives are quick-tempered and hot-headed. They boil much more quickly than most people. But it's soon over and done with, and they're usually

Figure 7–1. In backup, a person's normal style-based tendencies become more extreme.

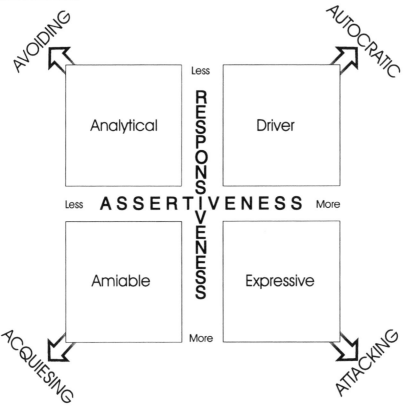

ready to let bygones be bygones. They expend their rage quickly and then it's usually finished.

In defense of their backup style, some Expressives admit, "Sure, I go on a rampage now and then and shout and pound the table and make wild statements. I get angry quickly, but I also get over it quickly." Other Expressives feel badly about having made loud and excessive verbal attacks that may have hurt someone's feelings.

No one likes to be the victim of verbal abuse. But people who are Expressives themselves tend to be more understanding of another Expressive's flare-up. Drivers can understand the Expressive's assertiveness under pressure but wish the Expressive would exert more emotional control. Both of these more assertive styles, though, may quickly put an occasional incident behind them.

The Expressive's outbursts have a more unsettling effect on Amiables and Analyticals. The Expressive's loud and loaded personal attacks may alarm these left-of-the-liners since the latter would have to be much more upset to launch such a blistering attack. Some of the wounding remarks are hard for Amiables and Analyticals to forget. Furthermore, left-of-the-line people are usually more judicious about what they say, even when they're angry. So they think to themselves, "If he said it, he must mean it. He wouldn't have said it unless he'd thought it first." Rash statements that Expressives make in anger continue to rankle left-of-the-liners long after the incident is past. The Amiables or Analyticals may also be upset at the blithe way the Expressive dismisses the incident after verbally blowing them out of the water. But Expressives, having gotten the stress out of their system, are soon ready to proceed as if nothing happened.

Drivers in Backup: Autocratic

Normally strong-willed, Drivers under extreme stress become very controlling; they try to impose their thoughts and plans on others. They seem utterly unbending, closed to any ideas but their own. When Drivers are in backup, they may express even less emotion than usual. Their eyes have a steely glint of determination but probably don't show much else. Not much given to gestures anyway, Drivers in backup tend to have a ramrod posture and may concentrate all their gestures into a vigorously pointing index finger. The voice of Drivers in backup may be somewhat loud and abrasive, or they may speak in an authoritatively quiet voice, like a resolute Clint Eastwood character.

In defense of their backup style, some Drivers say, "Sure, I may get a little autocratic when I'm stressed, but at least I don't 'lose it.' There's a task to be done, and I see that it gets done. I see no reason to apologize for that." Other Drivers, however, feel sorry that they've been so imperious and intimidating.

No one likes the uncompromising insistence of Drivers in backup that *their* goals be achieved, *their* plans be implemented, *their* schedule be followed, and *their* ideas carry the day. Plans conceived in backup are usually flawed. However, even when the ideas are sound, the insensitive and autocratic manner in which the Driver announces them usually provokes sufficient resistance to doom them to failure.

Other Drivers may at times overlook the dictatorial ways of a Driver in backup. Expressives can often understand the Driver's strong-mindedness (even though they may not like it), but they usually resent the unemotional facade put forth by the Driver in backup. The Expressive's attitude is, "If you're upset, say so! Don't mask your anger with this businesslike facade, with facts and figures!"

Less-assertive people are apt to be intimidated by what they consider to be the Drivers' "bulldozing" tactics when in backup. They resent feel-

ing pushed around and controlled. The normally fast-paced Drivers tend
to decide and act even quicker when in backup, which puts enormous
pressure on the slower-paced styles. Drivers' escalated attention to task
and, consequently, their diminished emphasis on people is especially
galling to Amiables.

Amiables in Backup: Acquiescing

In periods of low stress, Amiables are quiet, friendly, and cooperative;
they like to relate to others with minimal interpersonal tension. While
stress goads some people into shouting insults and others into rigidly
controlling behavior, the Amiables' desire to avoid conflict and appease
others becomes even more pronounced. They go overboard in appearing
cooperative and trying to minimize interpersonal tension.

It's often difficult to know when an Amiable is in backup. When an
Expressive is in backup, all the world knows it. And when a Driver is
highly stressed, it doesn't take us long to experience his or her excessively
controlling ways. But an Amiable slips into backup unobtrusively. He or
she may still be smiling and as agreeable as ever, even saying, "Sure,
that's okay."

While it seems as though nothing has changed when an Amiable
goes into backup, your first clue is often a gut feeling that something is
wrong, though you can't put your finger on the reason you feel that way.
When you observe the person more carefully, you'll note that, although
you're hearing agreeable words, the "music" of the body language has
changed. The tone of voice, facial expression, gesture, and posture are
mechanical and perfunctory, empty of commitment. If Amiables do put
words to their frustration, they only hint at it.

In defense of their backup style, some Amiables say, "What can possibly be wrong with being nice even when I'm stressed? Rather than make
a fuss or be overly controlling, we Amiables try to keep the peace." Other
Amiables realize that all backup styles, including their own, are stressful
to people and regret that their backup behavior may have been difficult
for others to cope with.

Expressives, who thrive on self-disclosure, dislike it when a person
feels one way but acts another. "If there's a problem," the Expressive
believes, "let's get it on the table and talk or shout it through, so we can
get beyond it. But don't act like everything is fine when it isn't." Drivers
have little patience with peace-at-any-price behavior. Analyticals can understand the desire to avoid conflict but dislike the way the Amiable who
is in backup goes about it. Analyticals find it distasteful when people say
things they don't believe, which is what they think Amiables do when in
backup.

Backup behavior is, by definition, inflexible. The Amiable's backup behavior often *seems* flexible—but in its own way it is as rigid as the backup behavior of any style. Perhaps you've sensed that an Amiable is upset. You may want to discuss whether you've done anything to cause that reaction. Even though it's obvious that something is wrong, the Amiable in backup generally says that everything is all right and is totally inflexible in insisting that there is no need to talk about the stress that's impacting the relationship. In his own quiet way, the Amiable in backup is as rigid and inflexible as anyone else.

Amiables' willingness to go along with what you want to do is based on a desire to avoid conflict rather than on a commitment to what's agreed on. Although genuinely supportive under normal circumstances, Amiables in backup respond with compliance rather than genuine cooperation. They say they'll go along, but they may not do what they agree to. In fact, the anger the Amiable feels but doesn't express directly may occasionally show itself in subtle forms of sabotage.

It takes longer for Amiables to move into backup than it does for the more assertive styles. Once in backup, though, Amiables tend to remain in that state for a much longer period. Though slow to anger, they are also slow to forgive and forget. There's no easy "Let bygones be bygones" for Amiables. As the poet Dryden cautioned, "Beware the fury of a patient man."

Analyticals in Backup: Avoiding

Like Amiables, Analyticals in backup try to avoid interpersonal tension. But Analyticals have their own way of coping with excess stress while seeking to avoid conflict. Analyticals are quiet, emotionally reserved people who generally prefer working alone to working with others. In backup, these tendencies become extreme. When Analyticals experience an overload of tension, they avoid both emotional expression and interpersonal involvement. Hence this backup style is referred to as Avoiding.

In the Avoiding mode, Analyticals, whose normal style is to be on the quiet side, say even less than usual. If they do speak, their communication is rational, factual, logical. Analyticals' vocal intonation, facial expressiveness, and gestures, all of which are normally understated, are even more limited in backup. In the process of becoming excessively rational and avoiding virtually all expression of feeling, Analyticals in backup withdraw emotionally from the people they are with. Though physically present, they are perceived as personally absent from the interaction.

Sometimes, emotional withdrawal doesn't give sufficient relief. Under those circumstances, Analyticals may try to avoid people and seek refuge in being alone. They may manufacture reasons for leaving a meeting or an appointment, or they may stalk out in a rare display of emotion. Thomas Jefferson, one of the founders of our nation, was an Analytical who at one point in his life engaged in major, long-term avoidance. He was so stung by the triumph of policies advocated by his rival Alexander Hamilton that he left the nation's capital and went home to Monticello. The future president of the United States canceled his newspaper subscriptions, cut off his political contacts, and for the next three years never went more than seven miles from his house.

In justification of their backup behavior, some Analyticals say that remaining unemotional when they're stressed is far better than making a scene. They also believe that when a person is severely stressed, withdrawal from other people is the best thing that can be done. Other Analyticals realize that they're not their normal selves when in backup and regret the negative effect their nonparticipation and emotional withdrawal have on other people.

Drivers, who like to tackle things head-on, are frustrated by the Analytical's avoidance when in backup. The more feeling-oriented styles, Expressives and Amiables, may be put off by the Analytical's normal emotional reserve. They strongly dislike the further emotional withdrawal that occurs when the Analytical is in backup. You can sense the frustration in an Expressive's comment, "I can deal with hate, I can deal with anger, I can deal with despair, I can deal with anybody who is feeling anything, but I can't deal with *nothing*."[1]

Analyticals' backup behavior carries a mixed message. Their calm and rational demeanor suggests that they're not upset or stressed. Everybody knows, however, that just the opposite is the case. They are highly stressed, but because they won't talk about it, no one knows why. This avoidance is frustrating to everyone, but it's maddening to Expressives who want to talk—or shout—things through.

Going Deeper Into Backup

After people shift into backup, their tension often decreases over time and they return to their normal behavior. However, if the stress continues to build still further, they are likely to shift into a *secondary backup style,* which is quite different from either their normal style or their primary backup style. While primary backup is an exaggeration or intensification of one's style-based behavior, *a person's secondary backup style is normally directly across the assertion continuum from the first backup style.* In terms of assertiveness, secondary backup is a reversal of one's typical behavior.

Figure 7–2 indicates the primary and secondary backup behavior for each of the styles.

President Nixon's Watergate crisis illustrated how people move from their normal style to their primary backup style and then, if the pressure isn't relieved, into secondary backup. Nixon's normal behavior could be characterized as more assertive and less emotionally disclosing than most people's. Under the stress of the Watergate investigation, he shifted from his normal Driver style into his primary backup behavior, Autocratic. For months he told people what they could and couldn't do and what he would and wouldn't do. But it didn't work. His stress continued to mount and he shifted into his secondary backup behavior, Avoiding. He retreated from the public eye and isolated himself from people. He refused to meet with his cabinet or even see his attorneys. His was a textbook case of a Driver who reacted to extreme stress by moving into his primary backup style—Autocratic—and then into a secondary backup style—Avoiding—in which he behaved in ways that were not characteristic of him.

It's hard enough for people to cope with you when you're engaged in the extreme behaviors of your primary backup behaviors. When you shift into secondary backup, people are taken by surprise because those behaviors are so foreign to you. Few people handle such surprises well.

Amiables in secondary backup are especially perplexing to most people. Their disposition is gentle and relaxed nearly all the time. In high-pressure situations, they move into their Acquiescing backup style. But every now and then, that doesn't relieve the stress. The pressure keeps building. When that happens, there's an explosion brewing. If Amiables reach their secondary backup, Attacking, they do it with a vengeance. There's yelling and name-calling. People are stunned by a personal attack from these normally gentle and courteous people.

Figure 7–2. Primary and secondary backup styles.

Style	Primary Backup	Secondary Backup
Expressive	Attacking	Acquiesing
Driver	Autocratic	Avoiding
Amiable	Acquiesing	Attacking
Analytical	Avoiding	Autocratic

Exceptions to the Rule

As you were reading about each style's backup behavior, you were undoubtedly reminded of your own or others' behavior. In some cases, the descriptions may not match your experience. As noted earlier, this approach to understanding people is based on probabilities. Most people's behavior follows the patterns described above. However, with backup behavior, as with everything else in this model, exceptions do occur.

Sometimes the exceptions are a response to one's environment. An Expressive in a corporate environment that frowns upon the kinds of emotional expressions characteristic of this style may be less attacking than usual. A Driver told us about how he grew up in a household where being autocratic was not allowed; his tendency under stress is to move directly to his secondary backup style, Avoiding.

Before assuming that you or someone else is an exception to the rule, make sure you look for the *early* backup behavior. What sometimes happens with Amiables and Analyticals is that the difference between their normal behavior and their backup behavior is so subtle that neither they nor their colleagues realize the Amiables or Analyticals are in backup. Then, when these Amiables and Analyticals go into secondary backup, they and others may think it's primary backup behavior since it's the first backup behavior they're aware of. So when you think there's an exception to the typical backup pattern, make sure you aren't mistaking people's secondary backup style for their primary backup behavior.

What is certain is that everyone's behavior is affected by excessive levels of stress. It's important to observe how you yourself and those you work with react to high levels of stress. Then you'll have information to help you figure out the most constructive thing to do when excessive stress begins to determine behavior.

The Good News and the Bad News

There's not a lot of good news about backup styles, but there is some and it's important. A backup style helps prevent stress from surging to levels that are dangerous to one's physical and emotional health.

It's widely known that while moderate levels of stress are beneficial, too much of it can cause sickness or even death. Stress has been linked to most modern ailments, from headaches to heart attacks.

Backup behavior is a protective device that helps alleviate dangerous levels of stress. Like a circuit breaker in an electrical system, it protects against damage caused by excessive loads. So your backup style makes an important contribution to your physical survival. Whenever you become frustrated with your own or someone else's backup style, it's important to remember two things:

1. The person is experiencing excessive stress.
2. The extreme, rigid, and frustrating behavior is a safety valve that helps protect the person from the ravages of dangerous levels of stress.

Although backup behavior may save your life, it can also get you into trouble. For one thing, when you are under the influence of your backup style, your judgment is severely impaired. Most decisions made under the influence of backup come back to haunt you later.

Backup behavior is disagreeable for others to experience. It's also highly contagious, and it can trigger a spiral of increasing alienation. When a person freely uses backup behavior with another person, that person is apt to become equally stressed and unconsciously respond with his or her own backup behavior. So now there are two people relying on extreme, rigid, and nonnegotiable behavior with each other in an escalating cycle of estrangement. Whatever your backup behavior, it's liable to trigger a spiral of increasing stress and counterproductive responses. That's why backup behavior often causes long-term damage to relationships.

Damage Control: When *You* Are in Backup

As powerful as your inborn backup reaction may be, you need not be at its mercy. Here are three things you can do to limit the damage.

First, eliminate as much excess stress as you can. Most of us know what to do; we simply need to do it. Here are some broad strategies for managing your stress levels:

- Do stress-reducing activities such as walking, jogging, swimming, listening to music, or watching a sunset.
- Temporarily moderate or eliminate some stressors by cutting back on your schedule or avoiding some of the people or situations that trigger a great deal of stress in you.
- Change the way you think about things. You can reduce your stress not only by changing the situation but also by changing your reaction to it.

Sensible as these stress-management strategies are, the very time they're most needed is often when it is most difficult to do what they suggest. As columnist Sydney Harris observed, "The time to relax is when you don't have time for it."

Second, *limit the interpersonal damage* that could be caused by your backup behavior. Reschedule meetings and appointments if possible. Even if you can't completely clear your schedule of meetings when you're in backup, it's important to postpone any that can be rescheduled.

If you have to meet with someone when you're in backup, decide to act temporarily as if you weren't in backup. A customer relations manager was having a hassle with one of her reps. The manager was clearly in backup and the interaction was deteriorating fast. The manager's phone rang. Although she had seemed uncontrollable only moments earlier, she talked normally with a customer for about five minutes. When she resumed talking with the rep, she once again resorted to the extreme and rigid behavior she had used before the phone call. Our point is that if she could use nonbackup behavior when talking to the customer, it was possible to have used it while talking to the employee.

We're not suggesting that you repress your feelings and keep your stress bottled up inside yourself. That's one of the worst things you can do. Instead, deal with your stress and your feelings—but in ways that won't damage your relationships. In other words, learn to dump your bucket of stress without filling someone else's bucket. Do your backup behavior—but not when you are with other people.

Finally, *don't make decisions while you are in backup.* If you do, you'll almost certainly come to regret it.

When in backup, stress clouds your mind. In that state, your instincts don't serve you well, either. When your two major decision-making resources are decommissioned, that's not the moment to make a choice you may have to live with for a long time.

Unfortunately, people in backup often feel irrational pressure to make decisions or take action immediately. Making decisions based on an abnormal pressure to avoid, acquiesce, dictate, or attack may relieve some pressure, but it's a very costly way of dealing with your stress. The purchase price of backup-biased decisions is usually a long-lasting set of negative consequences.

Obviously, decisions can't be put off forever. But the quality of decisions made by people in backup is so consistently poor that it's inadvisable to solve problems or make decisions while in that state. Rather than making poor decisions while "under the influence" (of backup, that is), it's advisable to focus on reducing your stress as quickly as you can. Do what it takes to get out of backup in as short a time as possible. Then make a decision of the best caliber you're capable of. Or delegate a particularly pressing decision to someone who is in full control of his or her faculties.

Damage Control: When *Others* Are in Backup

One of the most difficult interpersonal challenges you face is dealing constructively with other people when they're in backup. Here are guidelines that can help you make the best of a bad situation.

1. *Expect that people won't always be at their best.* The Roman philosopher Marcus Aurelius wrote, "Every morning when I leave my house, I say to myself, 'Today I shall meet an impudent man, an ungrateful one, one who talks too much. Therefore do not be surprised.' " He wasn't frustrated by people not living up to his expectations because he didn't have unrealistic expectations. The cliché is right: "Forewarned is forearmed."

2. *Detect when the other person is in backup.* It's usually obvious when the more overtly assertive styles—Expressives and Drivers—are in backup. However, with Analyticals and especially with Amiables, it can be difficult to spot the subtle differences between normal and backup behavior. Here are some ways of cluing in to the fact that someone may be in backup:

- You begin reacting negatively to that person.
- The other person's style-based behavior becomes more extreme or more rigid.
- In spending a lot of time with someone, you note specific behaviors that suggest when the person is in backup.

The sooner you determine that another person is in backup, the easier it is to deal with the situation.

3. *Avoid getting hooked by the other person's backup behavior.* As we've noted, backup behavior in one person tends to trigger backup behavior in others. To prevent this cycle from starting, reframe your thinking about what's going on.

Rather than focus on your dislike of the backup behavior the other is exhibiting, realize what lies behind it: an enormous buildup of stress. Try to shift your attention away from your discomfort with how the person is relating and toward empathy for all the stress the person is trying to cope with. You know how lousy it is to have so much stress that you're no longer yourself. Remind yourself that that's what life is like right now for this person who is in backup.

It's also helpful to remind yourself that you are not the real target of the other person's behavior. The offending behavior is a response to inner stress, and you happen to be in the way. So don't take it personally.

4. *Don't try to prevent a person from using backup behavior.* Backup behavior is a way of relieving stress. When its use is thwarted, the stress

overload is prolonged. Furthermore, when a person is in backup, your efforts to prevent the automatic stress-reducing mechanisms probably just increase the person's surplus stress.

Unfortunately, in our culture there is a strong tendency to urge people not to use their backup behavior. When an Expressive is in backup, people often say, "For heaven's sake, stop shouting, will you? Let's talk this over like two rational human beings." When an Analytical in backup becomes withdrawn, people often give their remedy, "Get it off your chest." When a Driver becomes autocratic and more intense than usual, people advise, "Relax, take it easy." When an Amiable is acquiescing, people may say, "Come on, be truthful . . . just say what's really on your mind." All this well-meant advice merely serves to increase the stress.

Obviously, when someone uses backup behavior over a long period of time, the situation must be confronted. If this needs to be done, wait until the person is out of backup before broaching the subject. You might help him or her develop tactics to prevent the buildup of too much stress. For example, review the person's workload to be sure that it's manageable and that there aren't too many deadlines that are too tight. Then, using information from this chapter, help the person devise damage-control strategies to use when in backup.

5. Finally, if at all possible, *avoid doing business with a person who is in backup.* The more important the business, the more important it is to avoid doing it when one person's interpersonal ability is impaired and his or her decision making is decommissioned.

Ray Kroc, the founder of the McDonald's fast-food chain and an Expressive, was under great pressure as the company grew explosively. Consequently, he was in backup fairly often. In his Attacking style, he often gave orders to fire the person he was mad at. At one time or another, he gave orders for virtually all of his managers to be fired. Few of his firings were carried out because his longtime secretary knew her boss would change his mind when he cooled off.

You can't avoid doing business with a person who is in backup. But when you know the person's backup style and accompanying idiosyncrasies, you can find a creative way of handling a difficult situation.

Since we're human, each of us will slip into backup behavior from time to time. The PeopleStyles approach helps you understand how you and the people you work with are likely to react when stress gets too high. It also offers practical guidance about what to do when you or others are in backup.

While knowing how to cope with backup behavior is useful, most of the time you and others are operating in your normal style. Even in less stressful times, it's a challenge to build good relationships with people whose styles are different from yours.

This wraps up Part One. Part Two shows how to create more productive relationships through the application of what you've learned about people's styles.

Part Two

Style Flex: The Key to Productive Relationships

You never know till you try to reach them how accessible men are; but you must approach each man by the right door.

—Henry Ward Beecher, *Proverbs From Plymouth Pulpit,* 1887

Chapter Eight

Finding Common Ground With People

You have your own way of doing things. You are comfortable with your ways of working and relating, and they work well for you most of the time. You've spent a lifetime creating these habits.

The problem is, the people you work with have their own sets of habits—different habits. When people of different styles work together but don't adjust to one another, serious problems can develop. Whenever people who work together don't get along with each other, communication suffers, cooperation diminishes, opportunities are missed, and productivity inevitably drops.

Sometimes a style clash is so bad that one of the individuals is fired. That's what happened to Robert P. Tyler, Jr., who was president and COO of Simmons Company. *Business Week* reported on September 5, 1977, that Tyler's boss, Grant G. Simmons, Jr., was "swift to make a decision, almost to a fault," while Tyler was "deliberate almost to a fault." Tyler was fired because of what was termed as the "incompatible management styles" of the two executives.

Our point of view is that although it's sometimes difficult to bridge the gap between different working styles, no style is incompatible with any other style. When people of two styles don't get along, the problem isn't incompatibility; it's usually inflexibility.

Getting in Sync With Others

Fortunately, working with someone of a different style doesn't have to be a disaster. People can collaborate powerfully when they capitalize on how their different approaches to work do in fact "fit."

Take Donald Peterson and Red Poling. In 1980, Peterson became president of Ford Motor Company and Poling became executive vice president. The automotive giant was on the brink of bankruptcy. That year,

Ford lost $2.2 billion, the largest single-year loss to that date in U.S. corporate history. Many analysts doubted the company could be turned around.

Despite the urgency of all the other things they had to do, Peterson and Poling set time aside to work at meshing their styles. Each had his style profiled. Each was coached on how to get in sync with the other's preferred ways of working. Capitalizing on their diverse skills and styles made them one of the most effective executive teams of the decade. They steered Ford clear of bankruptcy. In 1986, after six years of the Peterson-Poling collaboration, Ford's profits surpassed General Motors' for the first time in sixty-two years. In 1987 Ford's profits broke all previous industry records. That's one of the most dramatic success stories in U.S. corporate history: from the largest single-year loss to the greatest single-year profit in just seven years. Although many factors contributed to Ford's phenomenal resurgence, a major impetus was the way its top executives found common ground with each other.

What Style Flex Is

To succeed as a team, Peterson and Poling had to learn how to "flex" their style. Style flex involves tailoring your behavior so the way you work fits better with the other person's style. Flexing your behaviors is like a professional baseball player electing to swing differently at a fast ball, a slider, and a curve.

Flexibility, *Not* Manipulation or Conformity

People often develop mistaken ideas about what style flex is. They sometimes equate it with manipulation or conformity. There are practical, personal, and ethical reasons for distinguishing style flex from either manipulation or conformity.

Manipulation: Being Nice to People at Their Expense

In training sessions, when we talk about consciously adjusting our behavior to match the way another person likes to interact, some people get very upset. "Manipulation!" they claim in an accusatory tone. It's a serious charge.

The Random House Dictionary of the English Language says that to manipulate is "to manage or influence skillfully, especially in an unfair manner." Manipulation is being "nice" to people at their expense.

In recent decades many volumes have been written on the theme "manipulating your way to success." There are at least three reasons for not succumbing to this temptation.

First, manipulation is more likely to work against you than for you. Though the manipulator may reap short-term gains, the long-term consequences are negative. Sooner or later, people discover the deception. When that happens, the manipulator's influence evaporates, leaving suspicion and anger in its wake. People are doubly angry; they hate being taken for a sucker as much as they dislike having someone else gain advantage at their expense. Manipulators' reputations, which could be one of their greatest assets, are tarnished by their own actions. Their use of devious means ultimately costs them whatever influence they once had. As the saying goes, time wounds all heels.

Another drawback is that *to manipulate others is to harm yourself.* In his book *Man, The Manipulator*, psychologist Everett Shostrom wrote that "manipulation not only harms others, it is also *self*-defeating."[1] In a later book, he and his colleagues explained, "The truth is that to manipulate another is to reduce oneself to a 'thing' and limit one's potential for *human* contact. The manipulator devalues and thus defeats himself as a person by his manipulative action."[2] Fritz Perls, who founded gestalt therapy, put it this way:

> I call neurotic any man who uses his potential to manipulate others instead of growing up himself.[3]

To manipulate others is to diminish yourself. Why would anyone knowingly do that?

Finally, *manipulation is unethical.* It's an unscrupulous attempt to con people into bypassing their higher faculties of mind and spirit. In doing that, the manipulator treats other people as objects to be exploited rather than persons to relate to. But human beings are not things. As Dostoyevsky said, "People are people and not the keys of a piano." In a similar vein theologian Reuel Howe said, "God created persons to be loved and things to be used." There's a strong tendency, however, to do just the opposite. "Instead of loving persons and using things . . . we are always tempted to love things and use persons."[4]

The choice is yours. You can try to manipulate others with style flex or you can build honest, productive, mutually beneficial relationships with it.

Conformity: Withholding Your Point of View

A surprisingly common misunderstanding of style flex is that it implies the need to express the same opinions as the person you are with at the moment. Some people think style flex requires expressing conservative ideas to a conservative and liberal ideas to a liberal.

Is style flex just a souped-up version of spineless conformity? Certainly not. Applied behavioral scientists make a useful distinction between the *content* and the *process* of an interaction. Content refers to *what* is said: the information that's exchanged, the proposals that are discussed, the decisions that are made. Process refers to *how* people communicate: the intensity of body language, the loudness of voice, the amount of air time each person takes, and so forth.

People sometimes get the idea that style flex involves giving in to the other person's opinions or agreeing with their ideas. Nothing could be further from the truth. *Style flex is a way of adapting to another person's process; it is not about conforming to his or her point of view.* It is about relating constructively while appropriately disclosing your perspective on things as well as listening empathically to others. The better the interpersonal process, the more likely that people accurately hear each other and creatively resolve conflicting opinions.

When Amiables flex to Drivers, they don't alter the content they want to get across; they change the way they relate to the other person when expressing their thoughts. They pick up the pace of their speech, take a more factual approach, highlight pragmatic benefits, things like that. Choosing to change the substance of what you say is an entirely different matter from choosing whether or not to flex your style.

Style flex is not about giving up your goals or withholding your opinions. Rather, it entails presenting your ideas in ways that are comfortable to the other person. Not only is it possible to flex one's style while being straightforward about a difference of opinion, it's most needed in just that situation. When there's controversy about content, the last thing you want is needless stress in the process part of the interaction. When you create a more comfortable interpersonal process through style flex, you pave the way for constructive wrestling with the hard issues.

As is the case with manipulation, there are practical, personal, and ethical reasons for not withholding your own point of view on important issues. For one thing, *conformity seldom does much for you and often does a lot of harm, especially in long-term relationships.* One of the main reasons people conceal their own opinions is to get along better with others. Ironically, though, if you conceal or misrepresent your own stance to blend in with the person or group you are with, the relationship will deteriorate over time. Other people realize there's no point in communicating with you if you won't express your true opinions. It soon becomes obvious that they won't be able to count on you when the chips are down.

Then there's the problem of what to do when you are in the presence of people with conflicting opinions. You can try to remain silent, of course, but after a while many people will lose respect for you if you choose to sit on the sidelines when important issues are being discussed. As has often been observed, when you try to please everyone, you please no one. And, in the meantime, you lose just about everyone's trust.

Furthermore, *conformity is physically and psychologically damaging to the conformist.* When a person thinks one thing but says another, his nervous system takes a shot. Lewis Thomas, the noted physician, says, "We are biologically designed to be truthful to each other."[5] In *Doctor Zhivago*, Boris Pasternak writes, "Your health is bound to be affected if, day after day, you say the opposite of what you feel. . . . Our nervous system isn't just a fiction; it's a part of our physical body. . . . It can't be forever violated with impunity."[6]

Conformity also does a number on us psychologically. Nathaniel Branden, a psychologist specializing in self-esteem, says, "Integrity is, in effect, one of the guardians of mental health." He notes that when we behave in ways that conflict with our convictions, we lose face in our own eyes. We respect ourselves less.[7] It's bad enough when others distrust us; it's a psychological tragedy when we don't trust ourselves. Erich Fromm, the noted psychiatrist, stressed the damage to the personality caused by conformity. "If someone violates his moral and intellectual integrity, he weakens or even paralyzes his total personality."[8]

Finally, when important issues are at stake, it's unethical to refuse to disclose your real views. If a matter is important enough for people to care about what you think, it's usually important enough for you to speak forthrightly. If it's an issue that can improve quality, slash time, save money, gain customers, serve customers better, or give some employees a fairer deal, and if you have something to say, it's your responsibility to speak out. As the saying goes, "Silence isn't always golden; sometimes it's just yellow."

It's very important to distinguish between style flex and conformity. Style flex is not about pretending to agree with other people's ideas. It is a method for helping us disagree without being disagreeable.

Your Temporary Adjustment of a Few Behaviors

Style flex is your temporary adjustment of a few behaviors to improve the results of an interaction. We'll look at each of the key aspects of this definition since they contain important implications for flexing your style.

Style Flex Is Changing *Your* Behavior

Style flex is not about changing the other person; it's about changing yourself.

When it becomes clear that a relationship would work better if some changes were made, the question becomes, "Who will change—the other person or me?" People usually think it's unfair to change *their* behaviors when the other person's actions are a big part of the problem. Most of us believe that if the other person would change, the relationship would improve. In our quest for better relationships, we try to change our spouse, our kids, our parents, our peers, our manager, our reports, and others who are important to our happiness and success. As Mark Twain put it, "Nothing so needs reforming as other people's habits."

Trying to change others to increase compatibility only adds stress to an already burdened relationship. Ironically, the relationship can get better only when you realize the futility of trying to change the other person (unless the other person voluntarily decides to change). While this may seem like bad news, accepting the other person's style brings three positive outcomes.

First, you don't need to wait for the other person to come around to your way of doing things in order to get the relationship on track. You can do something now to improve things. *The primary leverage you have for improving a relationship is your own behavior.* Things look up when you shift the emphasis from "How can I get you to change?" to "What changes can I myself make?" Though you can't control other people's behavior, you can control your own.

Not only can you feel more in control, but your effort to adapt to the other person often enables you to achieve your goal. Fred Turner, who became chairman of McDonald's fast-food chain, learned about flexibility the hard way. When he first joined the fast-food franchiser, he was to evaluate the performance of individual restaurants in the chain. Turner's first evaluation resulted in "the most thorough report ever made on a single drive-in": a seven-page, single-spaced field service report. But McDonald's founder, Ray Kroc—an Expressive—wouldn't read the detailed report. The important information was useless until Turner condensed the material to one page and tailored it specifically for Kroc's use. According to John Love's history of the fast-food chain, the information in Turner's revised report did much to shape the future of that entire industry.[9]

The third benefit surprises many people. When you make it easier for another person to work with you, that person usually changes his or her behavior in ways you appreciate. As a result, both of you are now impacting the relationship positively. What starts out as a unilateral effort often winds up as a mutual contribution to the working relationship.

Regardless of who may be at fault for strains in a relationship, interpersonal flexibility involves taking the initiative for getting in sync with the other person. It doesn't matter whether the other person is your manager, a peer, a supplier, a customer, or someone who reports to you; you try to create ways for that person to work easily and productively with you. Your approach to each interaction is, "I'll do what I can to make it easy for him to work with me."

Style Flex Is Adjusting a Few Behaviors

Once you shift your mind-set about who's responsible for improving the relationship, you need to flex your style. Here, in brief, is how to do it.

First, detect the style-based differences between you and another person. Then adjust your body language and the way you say things to more closely match that person's preferred way of doing things. Carefully select *a few* types of behaviors to adjust—no more than three or four. Focus on what makes the interaction more comfortable for the other person.

For example, when Clark, an Analytical, decided to flex in a meeting with his Driver manager, Archie, Clark concentrated on changing two types of behavior. He knew his slow pace and focus on details often made Archie impatient. So, in that next meeting, Clark spoke more rapidly and focused more on the main points, bringing up details only when he thought it absolutely necessary to do so. Clark was amazed to find that these two changes in his behavior resulted in the best meeting he'd ever had with Archie.

People are often skeptical that a relationship can be improved by making so few adjustments. Yet psychologists Clifford Notorius and Howard Markham, after a two-decade-long research project on relationships, concluded, "Little changes in you can lead to huge changes in the relationship."[10] Our years of observation and experience support their conclusion: A limited number of behavioral adjustments can create major improvements. Try it and draw your own conclusions.

Flex Your Style Only at Key Times

As people learn to flex their style, some go overboard and try to flex all the time. However, there are dangers in excessive adaptability. Poet Carl Sandburg made this point with his story about the chameleon. It seems a particular chameleon got along very well for a time, adjusting moment by moment to his environment. However, one day he had to cross a Scotch plaid. The chameleon died at the crossroads, heroically trying to blend with all the colors at once.

As the chameleon discovered, flexibility can be overdone. People who overdo adjusting to others don't bring their own unique strengths to the relationship; instead, they lose much of their vitality. Rather than building rapport, their chameleonlike behavior often creates tension and distrust in others. People who aren't being themselves make others feel uncomfortable. That's why we suggest you consciously flex your style only at certain key moments. *Style flex is a temporary adjustment of a few behaviors.*

Now that you've seen what style flex is—and what it isn't—we'll focus in Chapter Nine on how and when to flex your style.[11]

Chapter Nine

Four Steps to Better Relationships

Gil Allen had a lot riding on the upcoming meeting with his manager, Joe Patterson, the executive vice president of their corporation. Gil had an hour and a half to present his division's staffing needs and budget for the coming year. If some new items weren't approved and increases granted for other items, his plans for the division would be hamstrung.

Cost containment was a major priority in this year's budgeting process. Not a good year to ask for increases. However, the new expenditures Gil was proposing would pay for themselves in less than three years. After that, significant savings would be realized each year. But all Gil's planning would be for naught unless he cleared the budgeting hurdle.

No one had ever suggested Gil's working relationship with Joe was smooth. Once, after a particularly tense encounter with Joe, Gil told his wife, "The interpersonal chemistry just isn't good." Through executive development, Gil learned a more useful way of describing the problem: He saw that he and the executive vice president had a clash of styles. Gil was an Expressive; Patterson was an Analytical. Neither was very flexible. Their my-way-not-your-way approach to working together severely hampered communication.

For the past four years, Gil's budget presentations to Joe Patterson had gone poorly. The more enthusiastically Gil waxed about his plans, the more detached Patterson got. Gil's colorful visuals received good reviews from some other people, but they didn't impress Patterson one bit. Patterson's disdain was evident in his remark that he could be "persuaded by facts," but he couldn't be "swayed by flash."

Two points made in the executive development session influenced Gil to take a different approach to the forthcoming budget meeting. One was that *how* a proposal is presented can be as crucial to its getting a fair hearing as *what* the proposal contains. The other idea that intrigued him was this: *When a relationship isn't going well, don't do more of the same; try something different.*

What Gil decided to do differently was to use his newly acquired skills in style flex in the crucial budget meeting. From the executive development session, Gil had derived a composite picture, tabulated by computer, of what five other people perceived his style to be. He identified Patterson's style and plotted both positions on a styles grid. Next, Gil asked Roger, one of his key people and an Analytical like Patterson, to help him figure out a better approach to the meeting. They settled on three things Gil would do differently in order to communicate better with Patterson.

First, Gil would "open in parallel." Instead of his usual way of trying to build rapport by telling a story, he would demonstrate more task-orientation. Gil planned to keep introductory comments informal yet brief and move quickly to the purpose of the meeting. It would be a serious, low-key beginning.

Next, Gil's presentation would be logical and thorough. It would be supported by a written summary and backed by extensive, detailed appendixes. Roger helped Gil develop the presentation and prepare the written report and appendixes. Patterson would have all the data he could possibly want. It would be carefully organized for easy reference.

Gil said, "I also decided to rein myself in more." He would talk less and listen more. Instead of immediately rebutting Patterson's concerns, as he usually did, Gil would encourage him to explain his reservations more fully. When he understood Patterson's frame of reference, he would acknowledge points of agreement and use facts and logic as much as possible when discussing their differences.

Gil and Roger both liked the approach they planned. However, Gil was concerned about implementing it. Though he was only making three changes in the way he would present, two of the changes were fairly encompassing; and they weren't things that came easily for him. So Gil and Roger role-played the meeting. Roger took the part of Patterson. The first practice didn't go very well. They discussed improvements and tried again. This time they were satisfied. Gil told Roger, "I'm as ready as I'll ever be."

In the actual meeting with Patterson, Gil felt he did quite well at flexing his style. As he monitored the interaction, he was aware of lapses; but, by and large, he was able to implement the plan. He was pleased with the outcome. Rapport was the best it had ever been in their meetings. Patterson didn't even make any cuts in Gil's budget. Gil concluded that the three behavioral changes he had made to get on Patterson's wavelength would come in handy in future meetings, too.

Style flex worked for Gil, and it can work for you, too. This is not to say that by flexing your style effectively you'll inevitably achieve your goals. That's neither possible nor desirable. If, by using a certain method, you could automatically get other people to do your bidding, their freedom as human beings would be destroyed. When we say that style flex works, we mean there's a high likelihood that rapport will be better and that your ideas will get a fairer hearing. If you listen more closely to the other person as well, the two of you will probably come up with a better outcome than if you don't flex your style.

If style flex is such a contributor to productive interactions, then the obvious question is, How do you do it? In this chapter we outline the steps of style flex. The four Appendixes delve into the specifics of what's involved in flexing to each style.

A Four-Step Process

For Gil Allen's meeting with his manager, Joe Patterson, Gil followed a series of steps.

> Step One: *Identify*. Gil knew his own style and identified Patterson's style.
> Step Two: *Plan*. With help from a colleague, Gil selected three types of behavior he could use differently to get more in sync with his boss. He knew that in the give-and-take of the meeting, it would be hard to do some of the things he planned, so he did a dry run with a colleague.
> Step Three: *Implement*. During the meeting with Patterson, Gil made the behavioral changes he thought would help him get in sync with Patterson's way of working. He also "took the pulse" of the meeting from time to time to see if he should make midcourse corrections.
> Step Four: *Evaluate*. When the meeting was over, he mentally reviewed the process and the outcome so he could learn from the experience.

Let's take a closer look at what's involved in each step.

Step One: Identify

In this step you:

- Note your own style
- Identify the other person's style

In order to flex your style, you need to identify it fairly accurately. Your initial self-assessment of your style may be faulty. In part, that's because your style isn't so much a matter of what you are like inside as it is about how you come across to other people. If you haven't received feedback on your style from others as yet, do it now, using the aids we provided in Chapter Five.

Obviously, to flex effectively it's important to correctly identify the style of the person or persons you'll be relating to. Accurate identification of the other person's style is so essential we've devoted Chapter Ten to style recognition.

Having pinpointed your own style and identified the other person's style, you're ready for the next step.

Step Two: Plan

Some people are turned off by the idea of planning how to interact with a colleague. More than one person has commented, "It's pretty bad when you have to plan how you are going to relate to a person. It's all so . . . calculated."

The fact is, *everyone* does some planning for communication with others. We create agendas for meetings. We sometimes note the things to be covered in a phone call. We know Helene is a "morning person," so we schedule an appointment with her early in the day. As we drive to work, we mull over an important conversation that's coming up.

We plan our nonwork interactions, too—even the most intimate ones. Before proposing marriage, many people spend considerable time thinking about where they'll propose and what they'll say. If there were tense words when we left home in the morning, we may try to think of what we can say or do to get the relationship back on track.

It's human nature to anticipate many of our meetings with people and to think about how we'd like the meeting to go. In the planning step of style flex, you simply incorporate your knowledge of styles into your preparation.

With experience, you are often able to do the planning in your head, on the spur of the moment, while you're talking with someone. At the beginning, though, or when the stakes are especially high, or when an interaction is apt to be quite stressful, it's best to do advance planning. Sometimes it's even advisable to write out the plan.

To help you plan better, we've created four Appendixes, to give people of each style specific suggestions about what to do when flexing to each of the other styles. If you are:

- An *Amiable,* turn to Appendix I, p. 121.
- A *Driver,* turn to Appendix II, p. 136.

- An *Expressive*, turn to Appendix III, p. 154.
- An *Analytical*, turn to Appendix IV, p. 170.

You may want to take a minute now to familiarize yourself with this invaluable resource.

As we've said, style flex deals mainly with the process of an interaction. Aside from process, you can often have a better meeting if you also plan a constructive approach to the content to be discussed. As you recall, Gil Allen did a good job of planning the content he would cover with Patterson as well as how he would attend to process by bridging the gap between their two styles.

Step Three: Implement

In this step, you are interacting with the other person, usually face-to-face but sometimes on the phone or in writing. As you relate to the person, you make those changes in your own behavior that you believe can improve the transaction.

As you flex your style, you monitor whether or not the changes you've made are having a positive effect on the interaction. Is this new way of relating helping the other person work more comfortably with you? Are you both being more productive? If so, your hypothesis is confirmed. If not, you can make on-the-spot adaptations to improve it.

A truly flexible person knows that when relating to people, a certain amount of trial and error is unavoidable. So do your best thinking about how to flex to a particular person, act on that plan, monitor the impact of your behavior, and modify both your plan and your behavior when that's indicated.

Step Four: Evaluate

Although the interaction has concluded, one crucial step of the style flex process remains: evaluation.

Whenever you flex your style, take a moment to do an after-the-fact critique. Over time, these brief evaluations can help you increase your style-flex skills and improve your relationships.

First, look at the results of the interaction.

- Given the content discussed, was the person more at ease than normal?
- Was the interaction more productive than usual?

Next, note what went well.

- What specifically did you do that the other person responded to positively?
- Which of your changed behaviors seemed to have the most impact?
- Is this something you want to do more often with this person?
- Is this something you'd want to consider doing with others of this style?

Finally, determine what disappointed you in your attempt to flex your style.

- What specifically did you try that did not seem to enhance the interaction?
- Was the problem due to:
  Misidentification of the person's style?
  Poor planning?
  Ineffective implementation?

The evaluation step also enriches your understanding of the four styles. When people first learn this model, they often develop a simplistic idea of each of the styles. A more realistic understanding of how the styles play themselves out in daily life comes from practicing style flex and learning about styles from each experience. As you mull over the ways the other person behaved when you were meeting, you gain a richness of understanding that can't be obtained any other way.

When to Flex Your Style

When should you flex your style? The general rule is to do it whenever it helps you establish or maintain a productive conversation. Here are some guidelines.

Not All the Time

By definition, style flex is the *temporary* adjustment of a few behaviors. Not only is it unnecessary to consciously adjust to other people's styles all the time, it's clearly undesirable to do so. For one thing, too much behavior that doesn't fit your personality may create suspicion and distrust among your colleagues. For another, the person who tries to flex all the time undermines his or her own personality. As two social psychologists wrote, "To be always 'on' would be to destroy ourselves."[1] You'll build better relationships if you flex on those occasions when it's especially appropriate and not worry about it the rest of the time.

Open in Parallel

It often makes sense to open in parallel, as Roger advised Gil. That is, flex your style at the beginning of a conversation to start out in sync with the person in question. This is a time for building rapport. Being in sync with the other person's way of relating is one of the best ways of getting off to a harmonious start.

Most people sense the value of opening a conversation on a favorable note. However, few people realize the extent to which the beginning of a discussion sets the tone for the rest of it. The climate that's established in the first few minutes is surprisingly durable. Sociologist Erving Goffmann, a specialist on human interaction, noted that shortly after a conversation begins, it's possible to predict how effective it will be.[2] That's why opening in parallel is one of the prime uses of style flex. We're not saying to open in parallel all the time. However, you can make the most of many conversations by getting in step with the other person at the outset.

Just-in-Time Flex

It's often a good plan to open in parallel and then, after a few minutes, relax your efforts. Keep monitoring the other person's stress, though, and if it starts to rise, begin to flex again. Then ease off after a few minutes. One manager we work with calls this "just-in-time flex."

When Something Important Is at Stake

Whenever an important issue is discussed, flex your style to help it get a fair hearing. Your style has a major impact on your communication. In fact, each style is partly a communication style. When you don't get in sync with another person's style, each of you may tune the other out on the basis of style differences alone. Many a good idea has been killed, not because it lacked merit but because the communication process doomed it from the outset.

Obviously, it makes sense to flex your style when you want to get your message across. It's also important to flex your style when others are trying to get their point across to you. Though *empowerment* is more of a catchy term than a reality in many organizations, the person who excels at communication—both sending and receiving—is increasingly valued by most corporations.

When the Other Person Seems to Be Under Considerable Stress

If you see signs of greater than normal stress in a person you're with, use style flex to avoid generating additional tension. To the degree the problem is style-based friction, your adjustments should correct the situation. Even if the stress is related to different points of view on an important issue, flexing your style should help.

When the Person You Are With Is Especially Rigid

As a consequence of their life experiences, some people are especially set in their ways. If you're working with an extreme my-way-not-your-way person, you have to work particularly hard at flexing in order to have a productive process and a positive outcome. By contrast, when the person you are dealing with is highly flexible, you won't have to put as much effort into flexing your style. Of course, you want to do your part in promoting good communication, but the other person is also doing much to bridge the interpersonal gap. Some of the most enjoyable communication occurs when two highly flexible people unconsciously make subtle adjustments that keep them in tune with each another. The conversation can be more like a graceful dance than a disciplined effort to get on the other person's wavelength.

Chapter Ten

How to Identify a Person's Style

Sherlock Holmes had been with his client for only a few minutes. Yet in that brief time he learned much that was missed by his companion, Dr. Watson. With feigned modesty the famous detective declared, "Beyond the obvious facts that he has at some time done manual labor, that he is a Freemason, that he has been in China, and that he has done a considerable amount of writing lately, I can deduce nothing."

Watson was astonished. None of these facts had been communicated verbally. How was it possible to know these things? Holmes reeled off the observations that led to his conclusions. The client's right hand was a size larger than his left. That suggested he once had done manual labor. The particular kind of breast pin he wore indicated that the client was a Freemason. The tattoo of a fish on the right wrist was of a type done only in China. Another clue suggesting a stay in that country was a Chinese coin dangling from the client's watch chain. There was a large shiny patch on the man's right cuff, and there was a smooth patch on the left elbow where it probably rested on the desk as he wrote.[1]

Style identification is a way of learning about people through observation. Observation entails more than merely watching what is happening. As Holmes once commented to Watson, "You see but you do *not* observe." Observation is focused and purposeful. It's an energetic search for relevant clues.

This chapter helps you sharpen your powers of observation. First, you learn how to separate observation of behavior from making inferences about the behavior. Then you learn what behavior to look for when identifying another person's style, how to fine-tune your assessment, and how to check your accuracy. The chapter closes with a number of tips for improving your ability to identify other people's styles.

Separate *Observing* From *Inferring*

Style identification is based on the observation of behavior. Behavior is what a person does that can be seen and heard. *Behavior is directly observable.* Behavior includes posture, gestures, and facial expressions as well as the words we say and the intonations we use. Behaviors are on the outside of a person, for all the world to see and hear.

Many inner qualities lie beneath the behavioral surface: thoughts, feelings, attitudes, motives, beliefs, values. *Inner qualities can't be observed.* No one can know for sure what's going on in another person's inner world. We can only infer, that is, guess at, what another person is thinking or feeling.

The distinction between observing behavior and making inferences probably seems very clear, and perhaps elementary, as you read it here. However, even after people have been taught the difference, *when asked to observe and describe behaviors, they often report their inferences.* In our workshops, for example, after distinguishing between observation and inference, the trainer carries out some specific behaviors and asks the participants to describe the behaviors they observe. For example, the trainer may stomp across the room, speak in a louder voice than usual, and vehemently shake a fist. When asked what behaviors they observed, most people tell the trainer, "You were angry." *Without realizing it, they are not reporting behaviors; rather, they are stating their inferences.*

When it comes to identifying a person's style, focus strictly on behavior—on what the person says or does. While you're observing behavior, *push aside the tendency to read meanings into what you see and hear.* Don't listen to the voice in your head that makes inferences. Don't make any judgments now, either. You may find yourself reacting to the behavior (liking it or not liking it). But put that aside and just observe, as specifically and accurately as you can, what the person is doing. Then place that information about behavior in your memory bank so you have the basic data to work with in the future. A key to successful observation is to be able to recall another person's behaviors without having your recollection contaminated by inferences about what those behaviors might mean.

What to Look For

Though few people realize it, all observation is selective. We have too much sensory data coming at us at one time to process it all. Communication researchers estimate that a person receives ten thousand sensory perceptions a second—more data than we can possibly attend to.

In response to this deluge, your mind selects, organizes, and interprets the many stimuli that are impinging on you at a specific moment. Whenever a sensory impression registers, it's because you've focused on it rather than on other data coming at you at the same time.

In style identification, you capitalize on this process of selective perception. You look for the specific clues that are most useful in discovering a person's style. Since style is determined by a person's level of assertiveness and responsiveness, you concentrate on clues related to those key dimensions of behavior.

Level of Assertiveness

Seven behavioral patterns, noted in Figure 10–1, are especially useful in ascertaining a person's level of assertiveness.

Seven categories are a lot to remember when you first practice style recognition. Actually, remembering just three words helps you identify important clues: *more, faster, louder.* Right-of-the-line styles speak more, gesture more, and demonstrate more energy than most people. They talk and move faster than half the population. They speak louder.

Or, you could remember these three words: *less, slower, softer.* That

Figure 10–1. Behavioral patterns that are useful for identifying a person's level of assertiveness.

Indicators of Assertiveness

	Less Assertive	More Assertive
amount of talking	LESS	MORE
rate of speaking	SLOWER	FASTER
voice volume	SOFTER	LOUDER
body movement	LESS, SLOWER	MORE, FASTER
energy expressed	LESS	MORE
posture	LEANS BACK	LEANS FORWARD
forcefulness of gestures	LESS	MORE

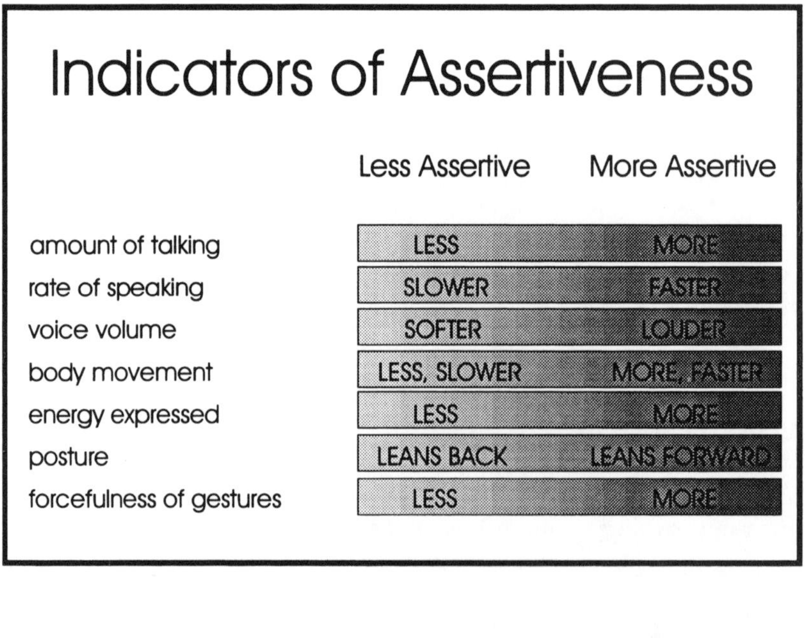

Figure 10–2. Simple yet reliable indicators of levels of assertiveness.

Indicators of Assertiveness Short Form	
Less Assertive	More Assertive
Less	More
Slower	Faster
Softer	Louder

characterizes *less* assertive behavior. Left-of-the-line styles show less energy and less movement, and they tend to speak less than the average person. They are somewhat slower-moving and slower-talking. They speak softly and their whole manner is quieter.

Figure 10–2 lists the three pairs of words that are the simplest guidelines for assessing a person's level of assertiveness.

Level of Responsiveness

Once you've gauged a person's degree of assertiveness, it's time to estimate the level of responsiveness. Does the person show more or less emotion than half the population?

Figure 10–3. Behavioral patterns that are useful for identifying a person's level of responsiveness.

Indicators of Responsiveness	Less Responsive	More Responsive
1. How much facial animation?	Less	More
2. How much voice variation?	Less	More
3. How "flowing" are their gestures?	Less	More

Since nonverbals provide good clues about the degree of responsiveness, be sure to notice the person's body language. More responsive people's feelings are quite transparent; they tend to wear their hearts on their
sleeve. You sense that you can read them. These emotionally demonstra-
tive people have more facial animation and vocal inflection than most
people. Their gestures and posture tend to be looser and more flowing
than average.

In Figure 10–3, there are three questions to help you identify a person's level of responsiveness.

You've probably picked up the similarity between the three types of
behavioral clues. Whether it's facial expression, voice, or gestures, *more*
responsive people have *more* variety and show *more* animation. *Less* responsive people have *less* variety and *less* animation in their facial, vocal,
and gestural expressions.

When you've determined a person's level of assertiveness and level
of responsiveness, you can make a tentative identification of his or her
style (see Figure 10–4).

Figure 10–4. Estimating the level of assertiveness and responsiveness
identifies the style.

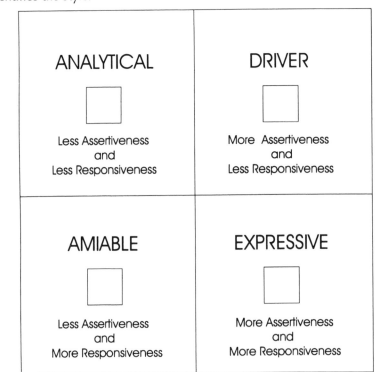

Review Style Clues

A person's style is more than just the level of assertiveness plus the responsiveness level. In other words, style is more than the sum of these two sets of behavioral clues. So once you've made a tentative identification of a person's style, check it out by reviewing all the clues for that style. The description of each style is found in Chapter Six.

Fine-Tune Your Assessment

So far, we've talked about determining which half of the assertiveness and responsiveness continuums represent a person's typical behavior. However, there are recognizable differences in assertiveness and responsiveness within each style. Thus it's often possible to determine which *quarter* of each continuum represents a person's typical behavior. That enables you to place that person in a "subquadrant" within their major style quadrant. When you are able to fine-tune style identification this much, you can do even better planning for style flex.

To do this kind of fine-tuning, figure out whether the person is more or less assertive than half the population. If he or she is in the *more assertive half*, ask yourself if the person is more or less assertive than *75 percent* of the population. If the person is less assertive than half the people, ask yourself if this person is more or less assertive than *25 percent* of the population.

Use the same process to determine what quarter of the vertical responsiveness axis best characterizes the person.

You now have all the information you need to determine someone's PeopleStyles subquadrant.

In Figure 10–5, notice that there's a miniature grid inside each quadrant. *When each axis of the grid is divided in half, there are four quadrants; when the axes are divided into quarters, there are sixteen subquadrants.* Each subquadrant has a two-word name. The second word designates which quadrant the person is in. That's the most important information, so we print the quadrant name in capital letters. The word designating the subsection of that quadrant is written with capital and lowercase letters.

Here's an example. In Figure 10–5, Sam Breen is an Analytical DRIVER. If you reverse the subquadrant names for Sam, you'd be putting him in a different quadrant. This can lead to mistakes in planning and can create misunderstanding anytime you talk about style with regard to other people. After a while, the naming process will be second nature to you, and you won't have to think about which name goes first.

Figure 10–5. The sixteen subquadrants.

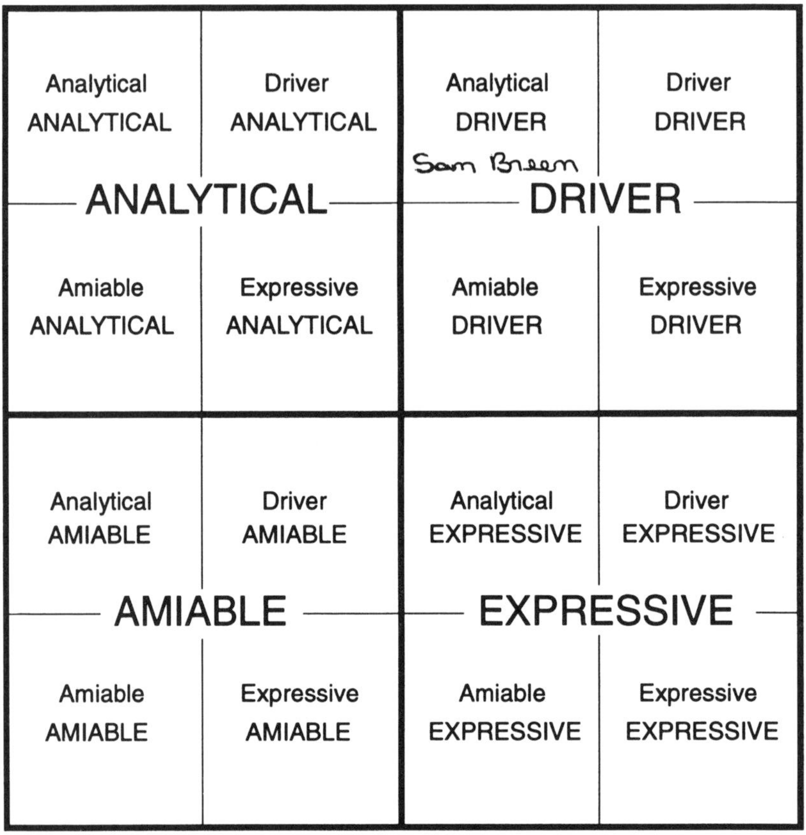

Analytical ANALYTICAL	Driver ANALYTICAL	Analytical DRIVER Sam Breen	Driver DRIVER
— ANALYTICAL—		— DRIVER —	
Amiable ANALYTICAL	Expressive ANALYTICAL	Amiable DRIVER	Expressive DRIVER
Analytical AMIABLE	Driver AMIABLE	Analytical EXPRESSIVE	Driver EXPRESSIVE
— AMIABLE —		— EXPRESSIVE —	
Amiable AMIABLE	Expressive AMIABLE	Amiable EXPRESSIVE	Expressive EXPRESSIVE

Although it's sometimes useful to know which subquadrant you are in and which the other person is in, that much refinement isn't always necessary. We are repeatedly impressed by how well we can relate to others when using the broad designations of "left of the line" or "right of the line" and "above the line" or "below the line."

Tips for Improved Style Identification

You now know the general process of style identification. Here are some tips that can help you do it accurately.

Make It Easy for the Other Person to Act True to Style

Although a person's style demonstrates itself in most situations, it is most clearly manifested when you demonstrate interest in the person and encourage him or her to take the lead in the conversation. If you come across too strongly with your own style-based behavior, the other person may primarily respond to your manner of relating rather than behave in ways characteristic of his or her own style.

Pay Attention to Body Language

Some of the best clues for identifying styles are nonverbal. Yet there's a strong tendency in our society for people to overlook the clues in body language. Train yourself to be more observant of people's gestures, posture, facial expression, rapidity and loudness of speech, and amount of inflection. We're not suggesting that you ignore verbal clues, but just that you give increased attention to the nonverbals.

Don't Be Misled by Style Labels

Labels are convenient, but they can easily lead to misunderstandings. For instance, when the word *Driver* is used, people may conjure up visions of a tyrant with whip in hand—even though some great humanitarians have been Drivers. Then, too, one of the most frequent mistakes in style identification comes from assuming a person is a Driver when, in reality, he or she is an Expressive. One reason so many Expressives are misidentified as Drivers is that the word *Expressive* doesn't seem to convey the high level of assertiveness that's characteristic of this style while the word *Driver* seems to do so. Some people think all highly assertive people are Drivers while actually half of these highly assertive people are Expressives. So don't allow yourself to be misled by the names of the styles.

Treat Your Initial Identification as a Working Hypothesis

Don't allow your initial perception of another person's style to be carved in stone. Continue to take in new information about the person's assertiveness and responsiveness: Check your hypothesis against specific clues about the style you think the person may be. Then test your hypothesis in action. Do that by flexing to what you believe is the person's style. If flexing your style in the way indicated makes it easier for the other person to relate to you, you've probably made an accurate assessment of the person's style. If style flex doesn't improve the relationship, you may have misdiagnosed the person's style. Keep observing and experimenting, and you'll undoubtedly figure out what you can do to make it easier for that person to work with you.

Knowledge of Style Is the Beginning of Wisdom About a Person

We are constantly amazed at how much the PeopleStyle concept has helped us better understand, relate to, sell to, and work with people.

When a person's style can be accurately identified, it provides a surprising amount of information about the person. At the same time, style pertains only to certain aspects of one's life. Each of us is far more than our style. Thus, identifying a person's style is only the beginning of getting to know that person. It is one step of what can be a long and exciting journey of discovery and appreciation.

Chapter Eleven

Too Much of a Good Thing

On a hot summer day, consultant Paul Mok, sprawled on Connecticut's Lordship Beach, was reading *The Count of Monte Cristo* by Alexandre Dumas. Suddenly he came upon a line that hit him with the force of revelation: "Any virtue carried to the extreme can become a crime." In those words, Mok found an explanation for the many people problems troubling his clients. He suddenly realized that the hundreds of executives whom he'd counseled were having interpersonal problems not because of their weaknesses, but because of their strengths. As Mok saw it, "They were overusing their strengths, employing them even when they were inappropriate, using them to the hilt—and beyond. And when used to excess, these strengths backfired—exploded in their faces.

In this chapter, we look at a potential strength of each style that, when overdone or misapplied, impedes results and creates interpersonal tension. Then we show what people can do to ensure that this quality remains a strength rather than a weakness. We conclude the discussion of each style with a list of some of the potential strengths that often become weaknesses due to overuse or misuse.

Driver's Strength: Forcefulness

The Driver is a mover and a shaker, a make-it-happen type of person. In the process of achieving their goals, however, Drivers may alienate other people. When they come on too strong, they may be seen as pushy, domineering, and authoritarian. They may run roughshod over the feelings and rights of others as they ramrod their ideas and objectives through, often causing resistance and resentment.

Antidote to Domineering: Listen Better and Speak Provisionally

There are a number of ways Drivers can moderate their forcefulness when it's more than others care to cope with. They can back off in pace, in pressuring others to decide and act, and in other highly assertive behaviors. Most significantly, they can listen better and speak provisionally.

You can't do much listening when you're doing most of the talking. To become a better listener, *cut back on the number of times you speak*. Using a ratio approach can be very effective. You can set an objective establishing how many times you do speak compared to the number of times you want to speak during a particular conversation. For instance, Dolores thought that in her meetings with Sean she was taking up more air time than was helpful. Dolores decided she'd speak only once for every two times she wanted to say something. Taking less air time improved their meetings significantly, so Dolores often used this "speaking ratio" when she met with Sean. As Dolores explained, "Sometimes I spoke twice in a row when I felt like it, but I was rigorous in sticking to the ratio I set. Sean's a very quiet person, so there were some awkward silences, especially at first, but it's working well now. It's easy to see that Sean feels better about our meetings, and he's raised a lot of important issues and contributed a number of good ideas—things he seldom did before."

When it's time to express your opinion, try expressing your point of view more provisionally. Dogmatic talk suggests that there's only one way to look at things: your way. "The right way to handle this is . . . " "Here's the approach to take in this situation . . . " Opinionated words, accompanied by an authoritarian tone of voice and manner, send this message: "I'm closed-minded. There's no point in discussing this. The true view has just been spoken."

By contrast, speaking provisionally enables you to jointly create a solution with others rather than impose your solution. To speak provisionally, you might say, "Another way to reach that result would be . . ." or "Here's an idea to consider . . ." Make your tone of voice and manner quietly assertive rather than domineering. The goal of speaking provisionally is to get an idea on the table, not to railroad it through; to cooperatively determine a course of action rather than to dictate what will be done.

If you find that your forcefulness is too much for other people, the most important thing you can do is listen more, and more competently. When you do say something, speaking less dogmatically and more provisionally helps you moderate your forcefulness.

Other Driver Strengths That Are Often Overused

In addition to their forcefulness, Drivers have a number of other tendencies that, when used well, are strengths. However, when overused or misused, they are weaknesses of the style. Figure 11–1 lists potential strengths of Drivers that become weaknesses when used poorly or inappropriately. Drivers can usually become much more effective and build

Figure 11–1. Driver strengths become weaknesses when overused.

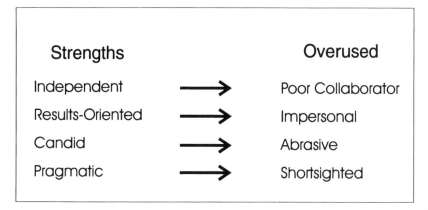

far better work relationships when they identify their points of greatest weakness and develop antidotes for them. Figure 11–1 is also a useful checklist for someone who is responsible for supervising and coaching an employee who is a Driver.

Expressive's Strength: Spontaneity

Spontaneity is one of the Expressive's obvious strengths. But excessively spontaneous Expressives can be difficult for others to work with. When Expressives do what they're drawn to at the moment, they tend not to deliver on existing commitments, whether it's their punctual attendance at a meeting or a project to be completed in a thorough and timely manner. After being let down by a string of broken commitments, people feel they can't rely on such a person to do what was agreed. Those left holding the bag are understandably resentful.

Antidote to Broken Commitments

There are a number of things you can do to avoid breaking commitments you've already made and to keep commitments that you'll make in the future. First, you need to constantly keep before you any existing commitments and record your progress toward completion. In addition to meetings and appointments, enter on your calendar the dates for the completion of milestones of projects. Figure out how much time is required to complete each milestone, and block out the needed time on the calendar. Many people find that their estimate of the time required to do something needs to be multiplied by 1.5 or 2 to account for snafus and unseen difficulties. Reserve extra time in the schedule for unexpected delays.

Sound planning is required to do this kind of calendaring. Projects need to be broken down into action steps. Barriers to completion of each step need to be determined and ways have to be devised to overcome each barrier in order to come up with realistic time estimates. Furthermore, although Expressives are people-oriented in many ways, they may not involve others in the planning of their pet projects. Participation takes too long for many of these fast-paced people. Besides, incorporating everyone else's input may so alter the original ideas as to cause the Expressive to lose all interest in the project. However, by not involving others in the planning stage, the Expressive may not get enough support to complete the project on time.

Being clear on one's priorities and relating all one's activities to these priorities also help an especially spontaneous person keep commitments. It's wonderful to be enticed by all the interesting possibilities embedded in new opportunities. But it's usually feasible to embark only on high-priority ventures.

Other Expressive Strengths That Are Often Overused

Along with their spontaneity, Expressives have several other characteristics that are strengths when employed effectively. When overused or mis-used, though, these qualities become weaknesses. Figure 11–2 lists potential strengths of Expressives that become weaknesses when used poorly. Expressives usually become much more effective and build far better work relationships when they identify their points of greatest weakness and develop antidotes for them. Figure 11–2 is also a useful checklist for someone who's responsible for supervising and coaching an employee who is an Expressive.

Analytical's Strength: Quality Orientation

A quest for quality is a major priority for Analyticals. If the pursuit of excellence degenerates into perfectionism, however, it becomes a liability. Perfectionists not only demand too much of themselves, but they set such high standards for others that no one can achieve them. It's very frustrat-ing to work with or for someone who will never be satisfied no matter how well you perform.

The compulsive perfectionist often sets lofty standards that go well beyond any functional purpose. Taken to the extreme, no task is so irrele-vant that it can't be redone; no report is so unimportant that it can't be revised again and again. This makes the perfectionist perennially late

Figure 11–2. Expressive strengths become weaknesses when overused.

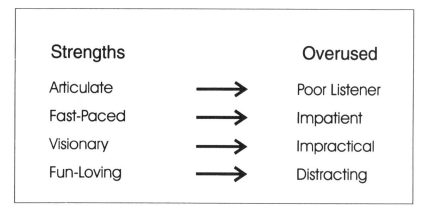

Strengths		Overused
Articulate	⟶	Poor Listener
Fast-Paced	⟶	Impatient
Visionary	⟶	Impractical
Fun-Loving	⟶	Distracting

with projects. In an economy where speed in decision making and implementation are increasingly essential to success, the snail's pace of the perfectionist causes innumerable lost opportunities. Perfectionists so focus on doing each detail well that they often miss the big picture. As Nicholas Thorndike warned, "You have to watch out for the railroad analyst who can tell you the number of ties between New York and Chicago but not when to sell Penn Central."

Antidote to Perfectionism: Commit to Timely Completion and Increase Compliments

Many negative aspects of perfectionism are overcome by committing to do things in a reasonable period of time and completing them on schedule. Analyticals who repeatedly miss deadlines need to create sound timetables and stick to them. Unlike the deadline-missing Expressive, the Analytical is often willing, and perhaps even eager, to create a detailed action plan with a clear timetable. Where the perfectionistic Analytical gets in trouble is in not sticking to the schedule he or she developed. In order to stay on schedule and meet a tight deadline, the Analytical who has something that's up to standard and will satisfy the end user needs to think "This isn't perfect, but it's good enough," and move on to the next task. When people are firm about deadline commitments they've made, they're forced to prioritize so that only those things that really require special attention receive it. When people who have been perfectionists start to deliver on time consistently, much of their relationship stress with colleagues vanishes.

It's also advisable for the perfectionist to say thank you more often. Most people perform much better at work and are far happier when the

Figure 11–3. Analytical strengths become weaknesses when overused.

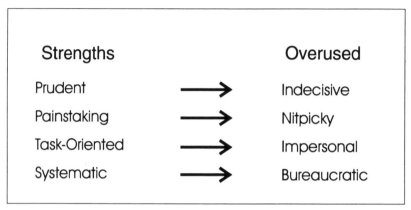

Strengths		Overused
Prudent	⟶	Indecisive
Painstaking	⟶	Nitpicky
Task-Oriented	⟶	Impersonal
Systematic	⟶	Bureaucratic

good things they've done are acknowledged. Perfectionists' standards are so high, however, that others rarely attain them. It's literally a thankless job to work for people like this since they're not likely to express appreciation until their high standards are surpassed. We're not suggesting that anyone indulge in insincere praise. We do suggest, though, that one of the best times to express appreciation is whenever people exceed their normal performance level in some aspect of their work, even if only by a little. So, if you are a perfectionist, don't wait until people exceed your incredibly high standards, but express sincere appreciation each time they inch above their current functioning in some part of their performance that you wanted to see improved. This process, which psychologists refer to as "shaping," helps you get the performance you want while improving your work relationships.

Other Analytical Strengths That Are Often Overused

In addition to their quality orientation, Analyticals have several other characteristics that are strengths when used effectively. However, when overused or otherwise misused, these qualities become weaknesses. Figure 11–3 lists potential strengths of Analyticals that become weaknesses when used poorly. Analyticals usually become much more effective and build far better work relationships when they identify their most serious shortcomings and develop antidotes for them. Figure 11–3 is also a useful checklist for someone who is responsible for supervising and coaching an employee who is an Analytical.

Amiable's Strength: Harmonizer

Amiables emphasize working harmoniously. People who overdo harmonious and cooperative behavior, however, tend to avoid conflict at almost any cost. They won't bring unpleasant facts to the surface, won't take a firm stand, and may suppress a conflict rather than resolve it.

In the conflict-avoidance mode, Amiables may sweep negative feelings under the rug. Ironically, while Amiables often try to maintain relationships by not speaking out, they're more often than not damaging those very relationships. People want to know what their co-workers think, even when they have a different point of view. An Amiable's lack of input may mean that others have to work harder at solving a problem. Or it may come across to others as if the Amiable is uninvolved in a team effort. Also, over time, people resent having to pull ideas and opinions out of a co-worker. By avoiding conflict, Amiables may not trouble any waters, but they usually diminish their standing in others' eyes because they haven't spoken their mind about crucial issues.

Antidote to Conflict Avoidance: Speak Your Mind

The first step is to know your mind. Some people can think on their feet and respond quickly to any topic; they know where they stand on whatever topic is raised. Not so with many Amiables. In the worst-case conflict scenario, Amiables experience a numbness about what they truly think and feel; if you were to ask them point blank what they think, they really couldn't say. More typically, Amiables get paralyzed by their ability to see the many sides of an issue. Taking a side leaves at least one party's needs unresolved.

As an Amiable, here's what you can do in situations where you might find it difficult to speak your mind.

Be prepared. If you're working with a new client, find out everything you can about the client. If it's a new process or procedure, read about it or talk to some people who are informed about it. Before a meeting, find out the agenda and the issues that will be discussed. Decide what you think about each issue and prepare yourself to contribute ideas about each topic.

Look for how issues or decisions affect you or the members of your team. You may not have a strong opinion about some issues; fabricating opinions is not what we're suggesting. However, many Amiables lose focus on how a decision affects their own time and work because they're considering how the decision impacts everyone else. To take everyone's needs into consideration can be very helpful. However, if you're feeling confused about what the best solution is, remind yourself of what impact a solution would have on you, your group, or your other commitments. That helps you know where you stand.

Figure out a constructive way to be assertive. Many Amiables who have a hard time speaking their mind are convinced that they can either be nice or be assertive—but not both. They hesitate to point out the weak-

Figure 11–4. Amiable strengths become weaknesses when overused.

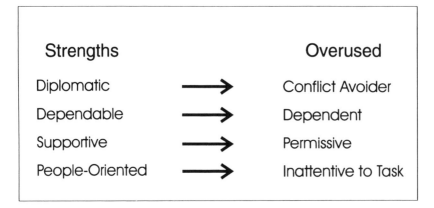

nesses in someone's idea because it could seem like a put-down. Fortunately, there are polite ways of being assertive that can play up to an Amiable's strengths. Usually, Amiables can see the good with the bad, so they might try saying, *"I like* your proposal that we get back to customers within twenty-four hours because it demonstrates a strong commitment to customer satisfaction. *I'm concerned* about how overloaded our customer service reps are already; we don't have the staff available to follow through on that level of service."

Other Amiable Strengths That Are Often Overused

In addition to their harmonizing behaviors, Amiables have several other characteristics that, when employed effectively, are strengths. When overused or misused, however, these qualities become weaknesses. Figure 11–4 lists potential strengths of Amiables that become weaknesses when used ineffectively. Amiables can become much more effective and can build far better work relationships when they identify their points of greatest weakness and develop antidotes for them. Figure 11–4 is also a useful checklist for someone who's responsible for supervising or coaching an employee who is an Amiable.

What Makes the Antidotes Difficult to Use

Each style is at risk for having its potential strengths become weaknesses. People who want to become more effective and at the same time build better work relationships undoubtedly need to change some behaviors. Antidotes like those described here help you flex your style in ways that can help you strengthen relationships with persons of *any* style.

Ironically, one thing the antidotes have in common is that they usually employ some of the tendencies of the kitty-corner style. That makes it a bit of a stretch to overcome the weakness. Even more of a barrier to using an antidote, however, is that the needed behaviors of the kitty-corner style are often behaviors that are disliked by the person who needs to grow in that area. They may be the very behaviors he or she deplores about the other style.

Ask an Amiable to be more candid, somewhat like Drivers are, and the Amiable is apt to be appalled. Amiables don't like the bluntness of some Drivers and distort the meaning of "being more candid" to "being brutally honest." If they stereotype an antidote negatively, they're not likely to correct their weaknesses.

The same aversion is found in the other styles. Ask an Expressive to plan and follow up on details more the way an Analytical would, and he or she is repelled at the thought. Thinking of the worst possible example of an Analytical, the Expressive will say, "What—you want me to be like Ted, confirming the same results six times? Forget it." An Analytical who is asked to be more outgoing with customers and employees may conjure up the image of an overly extroverted Expressive and say, "That's not for me." Or a Driver who is asked to listen more patiently to people may decide he won't "waste his time" listening to all sorts of trivia the way a particularly ineffective Amiable does.

Even though it's challenging to make the behavioral changes needed to keep your style-based weaknesses from doing you in, it's not nearly as difficult as most people make it seem. Often, the hardest part is working through the mental block to adding these particular behaviors to your repertoire.

We're not suggesting that you develop abilities characteristic of another style to such a degree that you would excel in them. Rather, our point is that if you tend to overuse some of your own style tendencies, your relationships and your general effectiveness will likely be improved by cultivating some compensating behaviors that are characteristic of the kitty-corner style. Don't try to excel at those characteristics. Just develop them to the point where your style-based weaknesses won't trip you up.

How to Know When You Are Overrelying on Your Strengths

At times you may sense you are overusing one or more of your strengths, so you can take steps to tone down that behavior a bit. At other times you won't even realize that you're doing too much of a good thing. It's like driving on a good road. Without realizing it, you're likely to accelerate more than you intended. Similarly, it's easy to accelerate some of your style-based strengths without any inkling that you've begun to overdo them.

To increase your awareness of using your strengths to excess, become more aware of how other people are reacting to you. As Goethe suggested, "If you want to know yourself, observe what your neighbors are doing." If your behavioral excesses are getting to people, you can probably see signs of increased stress in the persons you work with. Over time, you'll identify the reactions that people have when you overdo a particular strength. Acting on this awareness, you can moderate the use of those behaviors and substitute alternatives that feel better to others and work better for you.

Under normal circumstances people tend to have difficulty relating to others whose style is different from their own. When you begin to use style-based tendencies to excess, other styles experience even more difficulty working with you. Therefore, one of the best ways to improve your relationships through style flex is to moderate your excesses and substitute other behaviors in their place. Even when working alone, it makes sense to make sure you don't overrely on your favorite competencies. Whenever you overuse your strengths, they become liabilities that undermine your effectiveness.

Chapter Twelve

Flexing in Special Situations

Style flex is a way of tailoring your behavior to meet the demands of a situation. Other people's styles are important variables, but not necessarily the only variables to be considered. Participants in our seminars often want to know how to deal with style issues when other factors complicate the situation. In this chapter, we'll respond to six of the issues most frequently raised about how to use style flex:

"What if I'm flexing to my manager?"
"To employees?"
"To a group?"
"What if the person's style preferences are different from what's needed to do the task?"
"What if I can't figure out the other person's style?"
"What if I want to improve a relationship with someone whose style is the same as mine?"

Flexing to Your Manager

People often wonder whether to flex their style in meetings with their manager since the stakes are often higher in that relationship than in most others at work. There's more to lose if you try something and it doesn't work. However, it's unwise to ignore the way style affects this important relationship. In *Managing for Excellence*, David Bradford and Allan Cohen point out, "Subordinates can never safely ignore differences between their leadership style and that of their boss."[1]

Finding out how to flex to your manager is simple: *Just ask.* Say that you want to shift some of your behaviors to ensure that the way you work together is not causing him or her any discomfort.

Look for a good opportunity to have a discussion about style flex with your manager. It could be during a periodic progress review or a performance appraisal, at the beginning of a project or at a time when you are given new responsibilities. At one of these times when it's natural to raise the issue, ask your manager, "How would you like me to work with you?" Be sure to get specifics. If you're not getting clear-cut suggestions, ask such questions as: "How often do you want me to report on this project? On other projects? Under what circumstances?" "Do you prefer face-to-face interactions, telephone discussions, e-mail messages, or written memos?" "Would you prefer a detailed analysis, a brief summary with recommendations, or some other approach?" It often helps to use examples. "In my last report, did I give too much or too little information?" "How could I have presented the information in a way that would be more useful to you?"

After asking your manager for his or her preferences, shift your behavior toward them. Then, occasionally, check in to see how you're doing.

You may want to supplement what you've learned from discussions by *observing* your manager's preferences. Does your manager become impatient when people aren't on time? Is your manager's pace of movement and speech faster or slower than yours? You can observe how your peers interact with your manager and see what seems to make him or her more comfortable. You can also spot what doesn't work well.

Establishing a good working relationship with your manager can be a key to success in your job. Yet judging from the comments of the many people we've worked with over the past twenty years, we'd say the manager-employee relationship is often stressful and unpleasant for both parties. Although style flex is no panacea for the most difficult relationships, flexing to your manager's style can make that relationship more productive. Since your manager is one of the most crucial people in your work life right now, it makes sense to build a more effective work relationship by getting in sync with the way he or she likes to work.

Flexing to the People You Manage

Some managers are surprised at the suggestion that they need to try to get more in sync with their employees' ways of working. But it's an unusually good way of improving your employees' effectiveness and consequently your own productivity.

Most applications of the PeopleStyles concept to those who report to you are so straightforward as to require no comment. However, two things are worth emphasizing.

First, whenever possible, *give people the freedom to do things their way*. You'll never get peak performance from your associates if you expect them to do everything the way you'd do it. An Expressive sales manager kept trying to get all his people to behave like Expressives on their calls. He finally backed off when an Amiable on his team, who couldn't—or perhaps wouldn't—do things the manager's way, became the company's highest producer year after year.

It's common practice to try to change people's fundamental way of doing things. According to baseball great Graig Nettles, that's what the New York Yankees' coaching staff did to his teammate, pitcher Tommy John. "They tried to turn him into a power pitcher rather than a player who won with finesse. Here's a guy who's been getting by on what he's been doing for fifteen years, and they want to change him." John said he wanted out and was traded to California. Nettles concluded, "Tommy is as good a pitcher as he's ever been. He should still be pitching for the Yankees. It was stupid, all the way around."[2]

The route to success in sports and business is to encourage people to capitalize on their strengths by using their own style. The manager should help others develop into themselves at their best, rather than make them into pale imitations of the manager.

Second, when appropriate, *use style flex in team meetings.* In the next section we describe how to do that.

Flexing to a Group

In the course of a week, much of your time is probably spent in group meetings. If you're a manager, you meet with the people reporting to you. There are also meetings of the people on your managers' team, task force and committee meetings, and other gatherings to attend. How does style flex work when people of all four styles are interacting with one another?

When flexing to a group, follow the same four steps you'd use when flexing to an individual: Identify, plan, implement, evaluate. When working with a group, you identify the style of each person in the group. Then quickly draw a styles grid on paper or in your mind and locate group members on it (Figure 12–1). Once you've identified the members' styles and you've planned how to flex to the group, you implement the plan and then evaluate both the process and the results.

Here's how one manager used style flex to improve the performance of his team.

Al Lewis was manager of the information systems department for the northeastern region of a large manufacturing corporation. He consulted us because of his frustration at not being able to get his team of very capable managers to contribute many ideas at their weekly meetings. It was at these meetings that problems were noted, decisions made, and

Figure 12–1. After identifying the style of each member of a group, locate each person on a styles grid.

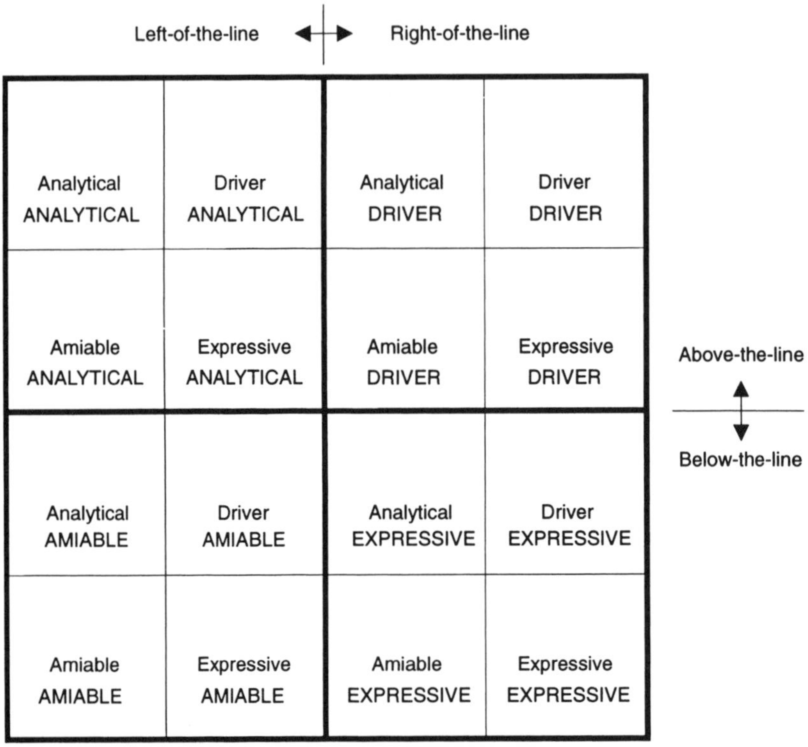

Left-of-the-line ◀┼▶ Right-of-the-line

Analytical ANALYTICAL	Driver ANALYTICAL	Analytical DRIVER	Driver DRIVER
Amiable ANALYTICAL	Expressive ANALYTICAL	Amiable DRIVER	Expressive DRIVER
Analytical AMIABLE	Driver AMIABLE	Analytical EXPRESSIVE	Driver EXPRESSIVE
Amiable AMIABLE	Expressive AMIABLE	Amiable EXPRESSIVE	Expressive EXPRESSIVE

Above-the-line

Below-the-line

action plans designed. It seemed to Al that he did all the thinking, contributing, and problem solving. No one else seemed willing to jump in with their reactions or their ideas, or even present their problems. Other team members confirmed that this was in fact the situation. Al wanted team building that would generate more participation in his meetings.

Since Al knew the PeopleStyles concept, he identified the style of each team member and located each person on a grid (as shown in Figure 12–2).

Identifying the styles of the team members, you recall, is step one of the four-step process described in Chapter Nine. Al then proceeded to step two, planning. He decided to flex only on the assertiveness dimension in his team meetings. He chose to make four changes:

1. Stop being the first one to give his ideas (as had been his custom).
2. Decrease his own participation by speaking only every third time he wanted to say something.
3. Use listening skills to draw out the ideas of others.

Figure 12–2. Members of Al's team located on a styles grid.

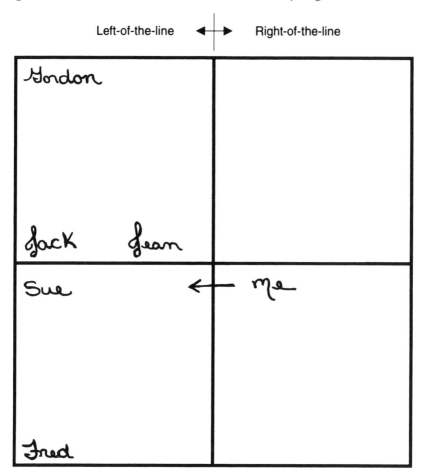

4. Decrease the number of items on the agenda so that there would be more time to discuss each item. The greater amount of time might be necessary not only to allow for more discussion but also to slow the pace of the discussion to better match the slower pace of his less assertive team members.

Al also planned to have a process observer at several team meetings to observe and give feedback on specific behaviors related to participation. Liz, the process observer, was to meet with the team once or twice before changes were made, so as to establish a baseline. Then she would serve as observer in several consecutive meetings where efforts would be made to increase participation.

Step three, implementation, was the tough one. Although Al was trying to modify only a few behaviors, he was going against the grain of a lifetime of habits. However, he did refrain from speaking first. He also talked only one-third as much as previously, and he used reflective listening skills. Data from the group process observer confirmed these changes. Al was amazed at how stressed he got and how tired he was at the end of the meeting.

Step four, evaluation, occurred at the end of the team's meeting and was led by the process observer. Liz reported that Al had generally done what he said he would. But there was almost no increase in other people's participation. The meeting consisted primarily of long, awkward silences. All members agreed that it was a terrible meeting. They hoped, however, that it was one of those situations where behavioral changes tend to make things worse before they improve.

The team decided to continue the experiment for four more sessions. One of the first signs that Al's participative efforts were paying off was when one team member said, "Al has done his part; now it's up to us to make some changes." Each member of the team committed to one or two behavioral changes in the next meeting. These were posted on a wall chart at the beginning of that meeting. By the fourth meeting, the group had hit its stride, and there was no turning back. The amount of team participation increased by more than 70 percent, the quality of the decisions improved (according to Al's assessment), and their implementation was more effective than previously.

Five years later, Al said, "It seemed traumatic at the time, but that effort at using style flex with the whole team had tremendous payoff. Our department has grown incredibly in the past several years. Our new mode of operation helped us handle the changes, and it readied my staff for the many promotions that have occurred."

Since every group is more than the collection of individuals who compose it, it's important to be able to flex to the group as a group. When you flex your style to the group you're in, there's much less irrelevant resistance to your input. And your flexibility undoubtedly heightens your team's productivity.

Flexing Both to a Person and to a Task

Sometimes what you need to do in flexing to another person undercuts your effectiveness in doing the task that the two of you are working on.

Here are some guidelines we've found helpful when the requirements of the task are very different from what's called for in flexing to your co-worker:

- First, build rapport by flexing to the person.
- When flexing to the person, don't use any behaviors that might be detrimental to achieving the task.
- When rapport is established, then flex to the task.
- As needed, oscillate between flexing to the person and flexing to the task.

This is how the process works in real life. Tony, an Amiable, was assigned to a project with Shelly, an Expressive. They'd worked together on two previous projects and had gotten on each other's nerves both times. After learning about PeopleStyles, Tony saw that much of the problem was due to their very different ways of working. This time, he planned to create a better relationship by flexing to Shelly's Expressive style.

The project they were to work on entailed meticulous examination of a large amount of information on customer purchasing trends. Detailed work with data is not a strong suit of Amiables (Tony's style), but of all the styles the Expressive (Shelly's style) is least suited for it (see Figure 12–3). Tony thought he was in a double bind. He was afraid that if he got in sync with his Expressive co-worker, the project would go down the tubes. On the other hand, he feared if he did what the job required, a key working relationship could be further damaged.

Here's what Tony did to complete the project successfully while improving his relationship with Shelly. In each session when they worked together, Tony "opened in parallel." He was determined to flex to those behaviors of his co-worker that could be an asset, or at least have a neutral impact on doing this particular task. He decided that in flexing to Shelly he would step up his pace by speaking, moving, and deciding faster and being more forthright about his opinions. He avoided joining Shelly's tendency to focus mainly on the big picture while giving only scant attention to details. Though that characteristic could be valuable in some situations, it would be very detrimental to this project.

Once rapport with Shelly was established, Tony flexed to the task. He was aware that they needed to have a good system for analyzing the extensive data. Since this wasn't a strong point for either Tony or Shelly, he suggested they ask an Analytical teammate to coach them. Once the system was in place, Tony and Shelly had to spend days at the repetitive and detailed work of inputting each customer's data. Predictably, Shelly soon got bored with the routine and the very detailed work.

When Shelly began to get bogged down from the monotony of the task, Tony realized he needed to flex once more to his co-worker. In addition to increasing the assertiveness of his posture and gestures and stepping up the pace at which he spoke and worked, Tony found ways to get in sync with Shelly's fun-loving side. He told a few jokes—a stretch for

Figure 12–3. What is required to do the task may be very different from what is needed to flex to the person you are working with.

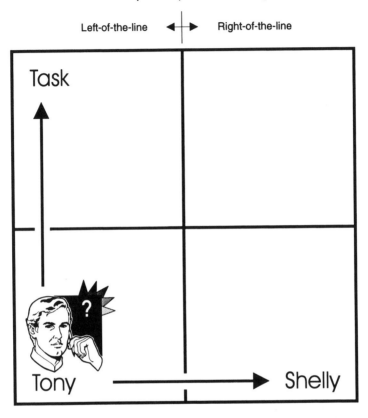

him—and found other ways to make the work more fun. Since this was not his customary behavior and was therefore taxing for him, he tapered off those efforts as Shelly again became more comfortable with him and with her work on the project. Throughout their work together, Tony monitored both Shelly's mood and their working relationship. When either condition needed attention, he flexed to her style. Otherwise, he concentrated primarily on working with the data.

It took a lot of Tony's energy to flex back and forth between his co-worker and the project. But Tony thought the results justified the effort. The project was a solid success, and the relationship was stronger than ever. In his words, "This project was far better than the other two in which Shelly and I got so stressed out with each other." Tony found that over time he became more adept at flexing to Shelly; on later projects, it took much less effort on his part to flex his style. Also, as the relationship became more congenial, Shelly became more open to Tony's way of doing things.

When You Can't Identify a Person's Style

There may be times when you want to flex to another person but are having trouble identifying the person's style. How do you proceed?

Even if you can't figure out a person's style, you may be able to peg his or her location on *one* of the two key dimensions of style-based behavior: assertiveness or responsiveness. Miguel, an Amiable, wanted to flex to Krystal, a co-worker, but he couldn't determine her style. It was clear to him, though, that she was more assertive than he. That told him a lot about what he could do to flex to her style. To flex, he could pick up the pace a bit, state his opinions more firmly, or try any of the other types of behaviors that would help him temporarily increase his assertiveness.

Many times when you can't recognize a person's style, he or she is located in one of the four central subquadrants of the grid. If you are in one of the central subquadrants yourself, there's probably no need to flex your style to someone located that near to you on the grid. If you are in one of the outer subquadrants, flex toward the middle of the grid.

Here are some other things you can do to flex when you're not sure of a person's style:

- Tone down some of your extreme behaviors, as discussed in Chapter Eleven.
- If you notice the person becoming stressed, make a guess as to which behaviors triggered the stress and modify those behaviors for a while.
- Do the opposite of what you normally would do. Thus, if you are typically quiet and unassuming, you might temporarily speak much louder and become more assertive and more demanding. If you're highly assertive, you might ease off a bit and let the other person bear more of the responsibility. If you are quick to express anger, tone down some of it when with this person. Or if you tend to keep your feelings to yourself, let them out a bit more. Doing the opposite of what you normally do is an approach that's often advisable when (1) the relationship is especially strained and (2) you've been unsuccessful in several other attempts to work more constructively with the person.

Relating to a Person Whose Style Is the Same as Yours

Throughout this book we've shown that style-based differences often trigger interpersonal tension. The similarities between you and a person of the same style can also become a source of friction, if they're not handled effectively.

Some years ago, we saw this dynamic played out week after week on national television. While President Nixon, a Driver, was in the White House, Dan Rather, another Driver, was covering the presidency for CBS. At press conferences, sparks flew as these two Drivers jostled with one another. Their relationship degenerated to the point that their interpersonal conflict was sometimes more widely reported than the substantive issues discussed at the press conferences. The animosity Nixon felt toward this other Driver can be seen by the fact that the White House placed Rather at the very top of its notorious hit list.

We're certainly not suggesting that the sole source of the conflict between Nixon and Rather was the similarity of their styles. But their conflict was typical of the way Drivers at their worst interact with one another.

For example, when there's a style-based clash between two Drivers, it's usually because they're both bringing high levels of assertiveness to the interaction. The solution is for one person to listen more, speak more provisionally, and try not to constrain the other any more than necessary.

When there's a style-based clash between two Expressives, it's often a similar problem. When there's too much assertiveness in an interaction, the same solution applies: One person needs to listen more, speak more provisionally, and try not to constrain the other any more than necessary. More than any style, Expressives love the limelight. If the conflict is about who will be on center stage, one of the parties may have to be temporarily more self-effacing.

When Amiables get frustrated with each other, it's often because each is taking the backseat, waiting for the other to take the lead. With no one in the driver's seat, there's no motion, no progress, no sense of accomplishment. The solution is for one person to exert more leadership—provide more goal orientation, more of an action focus, and more decisiveness.

When Analyticals irritate one another, it may be because they are so indecisive or so perfectionistic that they miss one important deadline after another. As the organization pressures them for completion, they may provoke one another more and more. The solution is to be more decisive and more pragmatic about the quality that's needed. Another problem that Analyticals can have with one another is that, more than any other style, these people have a need to be *right*. When that's the issue, it helps to listen better, speak more provisionally, and try to create a mutual outlook on what is being discussed.

A general guideline for what to do when you are in a style clash with a person of your own style is to moderate your behavior toward the opposite corner of the grid:

Driver: Flex toward the Amiable quadrant
Expressive: Flex toward the Analytical quadrant

Amiable: Flex toward the Driver quadrant
Analytical: Flex toward the Expressive quadrant

This chapter has shown how to apply style flex to special situations and to certain types of relationships. As you introduce the PeopleStyles approach into your life, you'll undoubtedly see important applications to such work activities as performance appraisals, delegation, coaching, goal setting, planning, time management, phrasing e-mail and voice mail messages, and so forth. We've found that the PeopleStyles concept helps us find ways to improve nearly every facet of our work life. It also has powerful applications for friendships and family relationships.

Thirteen

Three Keys to Good Relationships

We were puzzled. We'd been enthusiastic teachers of style flex for a number of years. We'd seen people make solid improvements in their work relationships because of it. Many told us about dramatic breakthroughs they'd made in formerly difficult work relationships. Others spoke of the powerful difference style flex had made in relationships with their spouse and children. Clearly, style flex was a powerful resource.

What puzzled us was our growing awareness that some people who became adept at style flex did not succeed in improving their relationships. We immediately investigated this problem.

Here's what we found. While style flex is a very useful way of bridging the differences between people's styles, by itself it's not sufficient for creating productive relationships.

A number of other factors influence relationships; through our investigation we relearned, for example, how important it is to relate to people the way virtually everyone wants to be treated. That's the foundation of constructive relationships. To be effective, style flex—or any other approach to improving relationships—must rest upon this foundation.

The Foundation of Good Relationships

The Golden Rule is an elegant integration of much of society's wisdom about human behavior. For example, Hillel, a Jewish scholar of the first century, addressed a key problem facing his people. At the time, pious Jews attempted to live up to 613 commandments—365 negative, 248 positive. It was impossible for the average person to remember all those laws, let alone obey them. Hillel's solution was to sum up all the commandments in a single succinct guideline: "Do not unto thy neighbor what is hateful unto thee; that is the whole law. All the rest is commentary."

This principle of human conduct is highly useful in settings where there is considerable cultural diversity. In fact, the Golden Rule can be found in one form or another in the scriptures of all the major world religions.

> *Buddhism:* Hurt not others in ways that you yourself would find hurtful.—Udana-Varga, 5, 18
>
> *Brahmanism:* This is the sum of duty: Do naught unto others which would cause you pain if done to you.—Mahabharata, 5, 1517
>
> *Christianity:* All things whatsoever ye would that men should do to you, do ye even so to them: for this is the Law and the Prophets.—Matthew 7:12 and Luke 6:31
>
> *Confucianism:* Surely it is the maxim of loving-kindness: Do not unto others that you would not have them do unto you.— Analects, 15, 23
>
> *Islam:* No one of you is a believer until he desires for his brother that which he desires for himself.—Sunnah
>
> *Taoism:* Regard your neighbor's gain as your own gain, and your neighbor's loss as your own loss.—T'ai Shang Kan Ying P'ien
>
> *Zoroastrianism:* That nature alone is good which refrains from doing unto another whatsoever is not good for itself.— Dadistan-i-dinik, 94, 5.

It's remarkable that people living in such different cultures would arrive at essentially the same summation of how to relate to people. The Golden Rule is as close to a universal guide to conduct as you'll find.

Many people wonder, though, whether this age-old precept is an effective guide in the tough environment of modern business. Fortunately, it has been field-tested in one industry after another and has often been associated with outstanding performance. J. C. Penney, who built one of the nation's largest retail chains, installed this tenet as a key operating principle of his company. As he was fond of insisting, "The Golden Rule is still golden." The philosophy of Worthington Industries is contained in a single sentence: "We treat our customers, employees, investors, and suppliers as we would like to be treated." Marion Laboratories' CEO, Ewing Kauffman, created one of the fastest growing and most profitable pharmaceutical companies by rigorous application of the Golden Rule. When asked why he applies the Golden Rule to the management of his company, he says, "It's just good business practice." The success of Mary Kay Ash's cosmetics firm in its first two decades astounded business analysts and competitors alike. She ran her remarkable corporation by what she referred to as "golden rule management." This guideline, one of the world's oldest and best-known prescriptions for relating to people, works wonders in today's complicated world of business.

How Virtually Everyone Wants to Be Treated

To gain a clearer understanding of how the Golden Rule applies to contemporary work relationships, we asked hundreds of participants in our PeopleStyles workshops to generate lists of the ways they like to be treated. We were astonished to find that in workshop after workshop, they usually gave the same three responses, and typically they were the first words out of people's mouths. People want to be treated with:

- Respect
- Fairness
- Honesty

We then observed those leaders who were exemplars in forging strong work relationships. We found that they demonstrated high levels of these attributes. Conversely, executives who had a number of troubled work relationships were usually gravely deficient in at least one of these qualities. In our workshops we began to emphasize the importance of these qualities, and participants found them to be key to productive work interactions—particularly in ongoing relationships.

We probed for what it means to be fair, honest, and respectful in one's relationships. Here's what we found.

Respect

Respect is essential to building constructive, ongoing relationships. Perhaps that's why many successful corporate leaders say respecting others is good business. As explained by IBM's former CEO, Thomas Watson, Jr., his corporation's approach to people management was based on "the simple belief that if we respected our people and helped them respect themselves, the company would certainly profit."[1]

Respect is based on the fact that every other individual is, above all else, a *person*. Respect is expressed through nondisparaging communication and by putting others at ease through using good manners. At its best, respect is the outer garment of goodwill.

Because the Other Individual Is a Person

People are sometimes surprised at the suggestion that they demonstrate respect for people they work with. Some protest, "A person has to earn my respect." Since few people live up to these folks' high standards, the majority of people they know are devalued. Those who don't measure up are often ignored. They're even treated with disdain and contempt because, after all, "They don't deserve my respect."

The kind of respect we're talking about has nothing to do with competence or incompetence. It's not something reserved for the deserving. Respect is what's due another person simply because he or she is a person.

In the workaday world, of course, a person's level of competence is very important. Underperformance must be confronted. If confrontation and coaching don't improve the performance, the person may have to be fired. However, even in the midst of difficult conversations about deficient performance, respectful treatment is called for.

Communication Without Put-Downs

Respect—or disrespect—is conveyed in the way we talk with people. It's not at all uncommon for people to feel put down by the way others communicate with them.

In T. S. Eliot's *The Confidential Clerk*, Elizabeth tells her husband:

> It's very strange, Claude, but this is the first time I have talked to you, without feeling very stupid. You always made me feel that I wasn't worth talking to.

Claude replies:

> And you always made me feel that *your* interests were much too deep for discussion with *me*. . . .[2]

What Elizabeth and Claude experienced at home also happens frequently in the workplace. Certain ways of talking and listening convey disrespect; other ways of communicating show respect. When another person talks, afford him or her the true courtesy of complete attention. When you speak, your manner can be collegial rather than patronizing. The highly flexible person is able to express disagreement without conveying disrespect for others or their ideas.

Using Good Manners

What people commonly refer to as *good manners* are really cultural norms—commonly agreed-upon ways of relating to one another. By defining what is appropriate conduct in many situations, these cultural norms make it possible for us to interact much more easily and efficiently. When we greet a co-worker in the morning, we don't have to figure out what to say or do. We can just give a conventional, "How're you doing today, Michelle?" She knows you aren't looking for an in-depth medical report or a detailed disclosure of her current mood. "Just fine. How're you?" is all she needs to say. Not a deep conversation—just a pleasant way to start the day.

The existence of cultural norms is a precondition of coordinated social behavior. Without agreements about interpersonal behaviors, we would not be able to run corporations or any other type of organization. These cultural norms are much more important than most of us realized when we were taught to say thank you to Aunt Harriet for a birthday present.

Cultural rules for relating to each other make interactions much safer psychologically—another reason why good manners are important. Psychologists have found that human beings are quite vulnerable psychologically. You probably know that from your own experience. But even people with strong egos may feel slighted, discounted, left out, put down, disliked, or rejected by other people. No one needs to be told how unpleasant those feelings are. Or that they seriously interfere with productivity.

Dr. Edgar Schein, an organizational psychologist, says that when you examine the cultural rules for social interaction, you'll find that their primary function is to protect people from being too vulnerable. Observing the social amenities helps people feel secure at a very fundamental emotional level.[3] As Jonathan Swift, the author of *Gulliver's Travels*, noted, "Good manners is the art of making those people easy with whom we converse. Whoever makes the fewest persons uneasy" has the best manners in the company.

What this boils down to is that when one person acts discourteously toward another person, the other is apt to feel uneasy and emotionally vulnerable. If this happens very often, you can bet that the person on the receiving end of the ill-mannered behavior will not be inclined to help the discourteous person succeed. That's why boorish manners are bad business.

The Outer Garment of Goodwill

It's true, of course, that some people's behavior gives good manners a bad name. Author Dorothy Parker observed, "Those who have mastered etiquette, who are entirely, impeccably right, would seem to arrive at a point of exquisite dullness." When a person's manners are merely an empty formality, they do little to build vital ties to others.

The spirit behind an action is usually evident in the behavior itself. There's a world of difference between mere politeness and true graciousness. Graciousness combines an awareness of social norms with genuine consideration of the feelings of others. It's a sensitive and creative way of expressing kindness in the ebb and flow of daily life. Graciously respectful behavior toward another is the "outer garment of goodwill."

Fairness

When we asked people how they want to be treated, *fairly* was usually one of the first words out of their mouths. To treat others fairly is to act justly and without bias toward them.

Unfortunately, well-intentioned people don't always agree on what's fair. What seems fair to people is often influenced by their situation. Ethical people may sincerely disagree on what's a fair wage if one person is a union member and the other is an executive in the same company.

Though there's no way to determine what would be absolutely fair in any situation, two questions can help you be reasonably fair in your dealings with others. First, ask yourself if you are using a win-win approach. In most situations it's appropriate for everyone to want to win. But the usual assumption about winning is that for someone to win, someone else has to lose. The win-win approach requires a shift in thinking. Instead of you *or* me, the emphasis is on you *and* me. The person taking a win-win approach seeks *mutually beneficial* outcomes for all parties.

After you've come up with what you think is a win-win approach, you can test its fairness by asking yourself another question. Immanuel Kant, a German philosopher and ethicist, taught us to test our behavior with the question, "Would I be willing to be the recipient of my action?"

Assuming that you are able to figure out what's fair in a situation, you still have to act on it. Often that's not easy because that means rising above self-interest or the interest of a group you are associated with. Being fair ultimately requires the moral fiber to be just and impartial when you could press your own advantage.

However, despite the difficulties involved, some people get a reputation for being fair even in difficult situations. Such a person, evidently, was Jock Conlan, a Chicago White Sox outfielder. In 1935 during a game with the St. Louis Browns, a base umpire fainted from heat exhaustion. Both teams agreed Conlan should take the base umpire's place for the rest of the game. He officiated, wearing his White Sox uniform.

Good relationships are forged by treating people "fair and square." That means seeking win-win approaches and making sure the scales aren't tipped unduly in your direction. It involves tough-minded impartiality when making the hard calls at work.

Honesty

True honesty is not something that comes easily. It's a rigorous moral achievement. George Washington once said, "I hope I shall always possess firmness and virtue enough to maintain what I consider the most enviable of all titles, the character of an 'honest man.' " The other most highly revered U.S. president, Abraham Lincoln, was known as "Honest Abe." Honesty is an important component of leadership.

Honest people *consistently* do three things. First, they steadfastly *refuse to make misleading statements.* They don't lie. They don't embellish the facts. They don't twist the truth to their advantage. They don't say, "The project is going fine," when it's behind schedule. They don't say, "Your job is secure," when they know it could be cut any month. When honest people make a statement, they believe it themselves.

Second, forthright people *do not withhold important information.* They don't conceal problems from their manager by a screen of silence. They give straight feedback to employees on a timely basis. Many people who abhor lying fall far short of true honesty because, for a variety of reasons, they don't divulge information that's important to others' success.

Honest people communicate the facts truthfully even when it's to their disadvantage to do so. This behavior may appear to be naive rather than honest. But we're talking about the tough-minded honesty of a person who is fully aware of possible negative consequences of telling the truth but who has the moral fiber to speak out nonetheless.

Finally, truly honest people are *genuine.* They don't seem to be other than who they really are. They don't put on airs. To use a phrase that was popular a few decades ago, "What you see is what you get."

Pope John XXIII elicited warmth from people of many faiths, in part because he was down to earth and lacking in pretense. The son of a peasant family, he never tried to conceal his humble origins. After being elected Pope, one of the first things he did was visit Regina Coeli, a large jail in Rome. While giving the prisoners his blessing, he commented that the last time he had been in jail was to visit his cousin. He never pretended to be a stained-glass saint. He was widely loved because, to an exceptional degree, he let the world see his real, unvarnished self. Time and again an astonished press described Pope John XXIII as "maskless."

Some people who are strong on honesty are weak on respect. However, the truly flexible person treats others with respect while saying what he truly believes. A person who did this exceptionally well was Roger Williams, founder of the state of Rhode Island and one of the strongest champions of religious freedom in colonial America. A vigorous advocate of liberty and justice, Williams called for better treatment of the Indians. He also spoke out strongly against the community's religious persecution. In letters to those who differed with him, he wrote his position clearly, then often wished his opponent well, stating his desire that the ways of God might be more fully disclosed to them both. A biographer says of this rugged pioneer, "His personal relations with men of all parties were marked by both frank controversy and friendliness. . . . Williams had learned the high act of carrying on a battle of ideas without loss of respect, esteem and affection."[4]

Through the years, we've become more and more aware that if we don't treat people honestly, fairly, and respectfully, style flex will not do much to improve the way we get along with them. When we are consistently honest, fair, and respectful with others, they learn from experience that they can trust us. *Trust is the most significant factor there is in creating and maintaining strong relationships.* This is the foundation on which all good relationships are built.

Strong relationships are built by being *consistently* honest, fair, and respectful of others. Being respectful only now and then, being fair only some of the time, and being honest only when the spirit so moves you is not a formula for building constructive relationships. These three qualities need to be an ever-present part of the way you work with others.

Think of what your life would be like if you were able to make your bad relationships good and your good relationships better. What you've learned about style flex when combined with being honest, fair, and respectful to others will do much to help you achieve that goal.

Most people who are introduced to this way of working with people find that it helps them better understand important dynamics of most of their relationships. The PeopleStyles approach provides very specific guidance for building better relationships. *Be sure to consult the Appendix designated for your style for guidance on specific ways of flexing to each style:*

- *Amiables,* turn to page 121.
- *Drivers,* turn to page 136.
- *Expressives,* turn to page 154.
- *Analyticals,* turn to page 170.

We wish you much success and happiness as you create more satisfying and productive relationships through sensitive style flex that's backed up by honesty, fair play, and respect.

Appendixes
How to Flex to Each Style

Appendix I

For *Amiables* Only: How to Flex to Each Style

The purpose of Appendix I is to coach Amiables on specific things they can do to create more productive relationships with people of each style.

Most of the recommendations are temporary behavioral changes that you can make just for a few minutes, before resuming your more comfortable style-based ways. However, we also mention a few options, such as goal setting, that have more long-term implications.

Since this appendix is a planning aid, don't try to read it straight through. Instead find the section that applies to the style you want to flex to:

- Analyticals, p. 121
- Expressives, p. 126
- Drivers, p. 129
- Other Amiables, p. 134

Read that section to figure out what you can do to make it easier for persons of that style to work effectively with you. Later, when you want to improve your relationship with someone of a different style, read the section dealing with that style. By working your way through the Appendix on an as-needed basis, you'll soon read all the sections and strengthen important relationships in the process.

Flexing to Analyticals

As an Amiable, you have much in common with Analyticals. You are similar on one of the two behavioral dimensions of style: Both of you are less assertive than most people. Consequently, Analyticals tend to appreciate your low-key ways.

In flexing to an Analytical, your major challenge is to get in sync with some of his or her less responsive behaviors. You can create a more effective working relationship with an Analytical by temporarily using some of the following four types of behavior, within each of which a number of specifics are mentioned. Do several, but not necessarily all, of the suggested specifics. You'll probably think of additional ways to work better with the particular person you have in mind.

Be More Task-Oriented

The Analytical is usually more task-oriented, and the Amiable tends to be more people-oriented. When working with an Analytical, you may want to give increased attention to the task side of things.

1. *Be on time.* Analyticals are more time-conscious than most Amiables. They expect you to be punctual.
2. *Get right to business.* Don't give the impression that you're there to chat. But don't lose your human touch, either. Limit the small talk. It's usually appropriate to spend a little time on openers, but keep it brief and don't make it too personal. Then get right into what you're there to talk about.
3. *Be a bit more formal.* It's easy for an Amiable to slip into a more casual demeanor than Analyticals may consider appropriate. Dress in a businesslike manner (assuming that's compatible with the culture of your company). Don't overuse slang.
4. *Maintain a somewhat reserved demeanor.* Amiables are friendlier than most people. But your Analytical colleagues are more comfortable with you when you maintain a somewhat reserved demeanor in your interactions with them.

Deemphasize Feelings

You can get more in sync with Analyticals by being *less* emotionally disclosing. Be more reserved without becoming cold or aloof.

1. *Decrease your eye contact.* Generally, Analyticals make less eye contact and are less comfortable with it than most people are.
2. *Limit your facial expressiveness.* Analyticals usually have a rather serious facial expression, especially when discussing business. In contrast, Amiables smile easily and often. To flex to Analyticals, have your facial expression be a closer match to your co-worker's seriousness.

3. *Limit your gestures.* Analyticals gesture less than any of the styles. Furthermore, feelings are communicated mainly through gestures and other aspects of body language, so when working with an Analytical, it may make sense to rely less on body English.
4. *Avoid touch.* Analyticals typically feel uneasy when someone touches them. Honor their preferences and avoid touch.
5. *Talk about what you think rather than about what you feel.* Think longer and harder about issues you're discussing with an Analytical. The words you use are important, too. Saying, "I think . . . ," instead of "I feel. . . ," can make a difference. Then follow with factual statements. Analyticals appreciate the change in conversational ambience when you begin using such phrases as "I've *analyzed* the situation . . . ," "My *objective* in doing this is . . . ," "My *plan* for the next quarter . . . ," "*A logical conclusion* . . . ," "Let me get some *more information* before I give my opinion on that." Why not use words and phrases that are music to an Analytical's ears?
6. *Don't upset yourself over the Analytical's impersonal and unfeeling manner.* If an Analytical seems distant or disengaged, don't take it personally unless you have reason to believe you've done something to offend. People of this style tend to be somewhat remote and unapproachable. Accept that this is the way these people are and that it's OK for them to be this way. You make things far worse if you create judgmental labels about them in your mind, or start telling yourself how bad they are or how unpleasant they are to work with.

Be Systematic

Analyticals like to be systematic about most things they're associated with. When you work with Analyticals, they find the relationship much more congenial when you are more systematic than usual.

1. *Set high standards.* Stretch as much as you can in setting standards for your work. Just be sure to deliver what you say you will. Analyticals get turned off sooner than most when someone makes a promise and doesn't deliver.
2. *Plan your work.* Analyticals are avid planners and like to work with people who develop detailed, step-by-step, written plans.
3. *Work your plan.* The Analytical thinks of a plan as a rational road to accomplishment—something that should be strictly adhered to. Consider being more organized than usual, without necessarily being as rigorous as the Analytical might wish.
4. *Develop superior procedures.* Analyticals relish outstanding quality. One way they try to achieve outstanding quality is through supe-

rior procedures and processes. When it comes to ongoing activities, they like co-workers to discover the best way of doing a task and then create a step-by-step procedure which, when followed, consistently yields excellent results. This rigorous attention to creating procedures doesn't come easily to Amiables. But you can do it. Chances are, you can find some areas in which new procedures are needed. As you develop them, you are likely to enhance productivity and build stronger ties to the Analyticals with whom you work.

5. *Continually improve procedures.* Even more than most people, Analyticals are concerned with continuous improvement. Support their quest for quality by improving some of the most important procedures in your area.

6. *Be more rigorous in following established procedures.* Analyticals tend to be sticklers for doing things according to set procedures. If you make the effort, you can probably think of procedures that would produce better results if you followed them more consistently. Doing so undoubtedly strengthens your relationship with the Analyticals in your work group.

Be Well Organized, Detailed, and Factual

Analyticals, the most perfectionistic of the styles, are particular about the way things are presented to them. They expect you to be well organized, detailed, and factual in your communication. In presenting ideas or recommendations to Analyticals, you make your case better when you incorporate the following behaviors:

1. *Be prepared.* Analyticals expect you to make good use of their time. Don't wing it; think things through in advance. Dig up all the data you need. Anticipate questions you may be asked. Even for one-on-one meetings, it's often appropriate to create an agenda. Consider getting the agenda to the Analytical in advance; she may want to think about the topics beforehand. Most of the suggestions below are enhanced if you give things more than your customary preparation.

2. *Have a well-organized presentation.* Explain your thoughts systematically. It often helps to present your ideas as a series of points arranged in a logical order. That's what Analyticals often do. You frequently hear them say, "In the first place, ... In the second place, . . ." and so forth. When communicating with an Analytical, do likewise.

3. *Go into considerable detail.* When making a presentation to people of this style, don't just hit the high points. Analyticals thrive on

specifics. They want to make sure all the ground has been covered before they make a decision. You gain credibility with people of this style when they see that you've chased down every detail.

4. *Give a sound rationale for narrowing the options.* Analyticals want to consider all the alternatives. While this tendency often helps them make good decisions, it also increases their tendency to be inordinately indecisive. You can help them weed out some of the weaker alternatives by giving them logical and factual reasons for doing so.

5. *Mention the problems and disadvantages of the proposal you put forward.* In addition to mentioning the advantages of the proposition you recommend, tell about the downside, too. The Analytical respects you for doing so. Then, further build your credibility by recommending ways of dealing with the problems and disadvantages.

6. *Show why the approach you advocate is best.* For Analyticals, "best" is a combination of quality, economy, and low risk. You have to figure out the relative weight of each of these criteria for the particular Analytical in the specific circumstances. "Best" for this style includes *long-term benefits* as well as immediate advantages. Discuss the future in terms of probabilities: "Here's a projection of what's likely to happen. . . ." Like you, the Analytical is conservative when it comes to risk, so if possible show why your approach is a fairly safe bet.

7. *Provide accurate factual evidence.* When talking with Analyticals, it's rarely advisable to use someone's opinion or recommendation as evidence. Hard facts persuade these folks. Since they like an objective presentation, avoid emotional appeals. Where others might settle for approximations, Analyticals want meticulously correct information. So be painstakingly accurate in what you report to people of this style.

8. *Stick to business.* Don't digress. As you discuss the business at hand and are reminded of things that are tangential to the discussion, don't pursue these side issues. When the time is up, depart quickly and graciously.

9. *Provide written support materials, and/or follow up in writing.* Analyticals tend to prefer the written word to the spoken. Even so, it's best to make an oral presentation as well. That way you can note the Analytical's reactions and answer his questions. At the same time, cater to the Analytical's preference for written communication by preparing well-thought-out support materials and/or a follow-up report. If a decision was reached, you may want to include a step-by-step timetable for implementation.

10. *Be prepared to listen to more than you want to know.* When Analyticals talk, they often present far more information than most people think is necessary. They explain their ideas or discuss progress on projects in what may feel to you like overwhelming detail. This much minutiae may be boring and difficult to follow, but be patient and stay tuned in. Analyticals appreciate your attentiveness. And, there's probably information you need to know buried somewhere in all that detail.

In your initial efforts to flex to Analyticals, you'll probably find it helpful to review the portrait of the Analytical style found in Chapter Six, pages 30–33.

Flexing to Expressives

As an Amiable you have much in common with Expressives. You are similar on one of the two basic dimensions of style: Both of you are more responsive than most people. Consequently, Expressives tend to appreciate your warmth, your friendliness, and your focus on people.

Your major challenge in flexing to an Expressive is to get in sync with some of her more assertive behaviors. You should be able to create a more effective working relationship with an Expressive by *temporarily* using some of the following five types of behavior. Within each type or category of behavior, a number of specifics are mentioned. Do several, but not necessarily all, of the specifics within the type of behavior you plan to emphasize. You'll probably think of additional ways to work better with the specific person you have in mind.

Pick up the Pace

Expressives tend to do everything at a faster pace than Amiables. Often you relate better to Expressives when you increase your pace to be more of a match for theirs.

1. *Move more quickly* than usual. Do whatever you are doing as fast as possible—on the double.
2. *Speak more rapidly* than is normal for you. Also, pause less often.
3. *Address problems quickly.* When problems arise, face them and dispose of them as soon as possible. From the Expressive's point of view, there's no time like the present to resolve a troubled situation.
4. *Be prepared to decide quickly.* Knowing that the Expressive makes decisions quickly, anticipate decisions he wants from you (or will

want to make with you) and do whatever preparation you can to speed your decision making.

5. *Implement decisions as soon as possible.* Once a decision is made, try to put it into operation immediately.
6. *Respond promptly to messages and requests,* in person or by telephone.
7. *When writing, keep it short.* Consider "bulleting" key points. Put supporting information in appendixes. Expressives like to keep paperwork at a minimum.
8. *Expect the hurry-up-and-wait phenomenon.* The fast-paced Expressive wants things done yesterday. But after you've knocked yourself out and met the Expressive's deadline, your work may be ignored for some time as the Expressive takes up another project. Your project, which seemed so urgently needed a short time ago, may gather dust for a few months. It's important not to take these incidents personally. Realize that it's a style-based tendency. On the other hand, if you experience a great deal of hurry-up-and-wait with a particular person, be sure to confront the issue.

Demonstrate Higher Energy

Expressives are high-energy people. When relating to Expressives, there are times when you need to put more vigor into what you say and do.

1. *Maintain an erect posture.* Keep your back straight and lean into the conversation. Keep your head erect, not propped on your hands.
2. *Use gestures to show your involvement in the conversation.* Use larger motions. Be more emphatic with body English.
3. *Increase the frequency and intensity of your eye contact.*
4. *Increase your vocal intensity.* Speak louder than you normally would. Let the intensity of your voice communicate that you are taking the matter seriously. Show conviction through your voice.
5. *Move and speak more quickly.* The behaviors that were mentioned under the heading "Pick Up the Pace" all help you interact more energetically.

Focus on the Big Picture

Expressives want to take a macro view of things. They quickly become impatient when a discussion turns to the nitty-gritty. In fact, of all the styles Expressives are the least interested in details. Although as an Amiable you aren't nearly as detail-oriented as Analyticals, there are times when you wish to discuss more particulars than the Expressive cares to.

1. *Concentrate on high-priority issues.* You probably have a lot more topics you want to talk about than the Expressive wants to hear about. When briefing an Expressive, radically prune the list of items to discuss.
2. *Present the main points and skip all but the most essential details.* Expressives rarely feel they need anything more than an overview. They will ask for more information if they want it.
3. *Nevertheless, make sure the details are well attended to.* While Expressives are not particularly interested in hearing about the nitty-gritty that you have to concentrate on, they can become very impatient if someone's inattention to details causes them problems.

Say What You Think

Expressives speak candidly and directly. Amiables are apt to keep their thoughts to themselves and speak somewhat tentatively and indirectly. Here's how you can bridge that behavioral gap.

1. *Speak up more often.* Initiate more conversations. In discussions and meetings, express yourself frequently enough so there's a more balanced give-and-take. Expressives usually want to know where people stand. They would rather not have to try to interpret the meaning of your silence or have to pry thoughts out of you.
2. *Tell more; ask less.* Say "Here's what I think . . . ," rather than "Do you think it would make sense to . . . ?" Say "Please do this" instead of "Could you do this?"
3. *Make statements that are definite rather than tentative.* Avoid words like *try, perhaps, maybe, possibly,* etc. Be specific. Don't say you'll complete a project "as soon as possible": Say it will be done "by twelve noon next Tuesday."
4. *Eliminate gestures that suggest you lack confidence in the point you are making.* Don't shrug your shoulders, hold your palms up, or use facial expressions that undercut what you are saying, imply helplessness, or suggest the avoidance of responsibility.
5. *Voice your disagreements.* When Expressives disagree with you, they usually come right out and say so. They expect the same from you. Face conflict more openly. State your opinions frankly but tactfully. At the same time, try to avoid situations where you and the Expressive are battling from entrenched positions. If it gets to that point, the highly competitive Expressive may put more emphasis on winning the argument than on arriving at a common understanding.
6. *Recommend a course of action and sell it with enthusiasm.* Expressives like to be pumped up about the choices they make and the things

they do. A careful weighing of the pros and cons of numerous alternatives rarely gives the Expressive the excitement she expects from making a decision. So when it's appropriate, make a specific recommendation. Integrity requires you to mention the disadvantages, but when you can do so with a clear conscience, emphasize the positives. Pull out all the stops; Expressives usually like an emotional appeal.

7. *Don't gloss over problems.* Expressives will be furious if they hear from others what they should hear from you. Beat bad news to the punch. Then give regular, frank reports on your progress regarding the problem situation.

Facilitate Self-Determination

Expressives like to set their own direction. They want to do things their way. Here are some ways Amiables can constructively facilitate an Expressive's sense of self-direction.

1. *Give Expressives as much freedom as possible in achieving their visions.*
2. *As far as practicable, let the Expressive determine how to do projects and achieve objectives.*
3. *Don't be a stickler for rules.* Expressives are prone to stretch or break rules in order to achieve results. Be open to changing or bending the rules when appropriate.

In your initial efforts to flex to Expressives, you'll probably find it helpful to review the portrait of the Expressive style found in Chapter Six, pages 38–43.

Flexing to Drivers

As an Amiable you differ from the Driver on both of the basic dimensions of style: The Driver is more assertive and less responsive than you are. Thus you experience more style-based differences with Drivers than with either Analyticals or Expressives, each of which has one basic dimension of behavior in common with you. As a result you find more types of behavior you can modify when flexing to a Driver than when flexing to any other style.

As you read the types of temporary adjustment of behavior that help you get in sync with Drivers, select carefully the one to four types you think will help you work best with a particular person. It's not easy to change habitual behavior, even for a short time, so be sure to select only one to four types of behavior to work on. Within each type or category of behavior, a number of specifics are mentioned. Do several, but not necessarily all, of the specifics within the behavioral category you plan to emphasize. You'll probably think of additional ways to work better with the specific person you have in mind.

Pick up the Pace

Drivers tend to do everything at a fast pace. You often relate better to Drivers when you increase your pace considerably.

1. *Move more quickly than usual.* Walk at a faster pace. Do whatever you are doing as quickly as possible—on the double when you flex to a Driver.
2. *Speak more rapidly than is normal for you.* Also, pause less often.
3. *Use time efficiently.* When meeting with a Driver, don't exceed the allotted time. Do your business at a fast clip. Then leave quickly yet graciously.
4. *Address problems quickly.* When problems arise, face them and dispose of them as soon as possible. From the Driver's point of view, there's no time like the present to resolve a troubled situation.
5. *Be prepared to decide quickly.* Knowing that the Driver makes decisions quickly, anticipate decisions she wants from you (or will want to make with you) and do whatever preparation you can to speed your decision making.
6. *Implement decisions as soon as possible.* Once a decision is made, try to put it into operation immediately. Drivers are do-it-now people. When you are action-oriented, they're less stressed.
7. *Complete projects on schedule.* More than any other style, Drivers value on-time completion. Don't be casual about deadlines. When you commit to a schedule, especially with a Driver, keep your commitment.
8. *Respond promptly to messages and requests.*
9. *When writing, keep it short.* Consider "bulleting" key points. Put supporting information in appendixes.

Demonstrate Higher Energy

Drivers are typically high-energy people. When relating to Drivers, there are times when you'll need to put more vigor into what you say and do.

1. *Maintain an erect posture.* Keep your back straight and lean into the conversation. Keep your feet flat on the floor. Keep your head erect, not propped on your hands.
2. *Use gestures to show your involvement in the conversation.* As an Ami-

able, you tend to use loose, flowing gestures. Use more emphatic body English.

3. *Increase the frequency and intensity of your eye contact.*
4. *Increase your vocal intensity.* Speak a bit louder than you normally would. Let the intensity of your voice communicate that you are taking the matter seriously. Show conviction through your voice.
5. *Move and speak more quickly.* The behaviors that were mentioned under the heading "Pick Up the Pace" all help you interact more energetically.

Be More Task-Oriented

The Driver is usually more task-oriented and the Amiable tends to be more people-oriented. When working with a Driver, you may want to give increased attention to the task side of things.

1. *Be on time.* Drivers are more time-conscious than most Amiables. They expect you to be punctual.
2. *Get right to business.* Don't give the impression that you're there to chat. But don't lose your human touch, either. Limit the small talk. It's usually appropriate to spend a little time on openers, but keep it brief and don't make it too personal. Then get right into what you're there to talk about.
3. *Be a bit more formal.* It's easy for an Amiable to slip into a more casual demeanor than Drivers may consider appropriate. Dress in a businesslike manner (assuming that that's compatible with the culture of your company).
4. *Maintain a businesslike demeanor.* Drivers prefer to keep focused on the task.

Deemphasize Feelings

Drivers are less emotionally aware and less disclosing of their feelings than most people. You can get more in sync with Drivers by being less emotionally disclosing. Be more reserved without becoming cold or aloof.

1. *Limit your facial expressiveness.* To flex to Drivers, have your facial expression be a closer match to your co-worker's seriousness.
2. *Limit your gestures.* When working with a Driver, it usually makes sense to rely less on body English. Talk less with your hands, for example.
3. *Avoid touch.* Below-the-line people, including many Amiables, spontaneously reach out and touch the person they're talking to.

Drivers typically feel uneasy when someone touches them. Honor their preferences and avoid touch.

4. *Talk about what you think rather than about what you feel. Think* about issues you'll be discussing with a Driver. The words you use are important, too. Saying *"I think . . ."* instead of *"I feel . . ."* can make a difference. Then follow up with factual statements. Drivers appreciate the change in conversational ambience when you begin using such phrases as "I've *analyzed* the situation . . . ," "My *objective* in doing this is . . . ," "My *plan* for the next quarter . . . ," "A *logical conclusion* . . . ," Why not use words and phrases that are music to a Driver's ears?

5. *Don't upset yourself if the Driver seems impersonal.* These people are so focused on task and are so time-conscious that you may feel you are just another piece of equipment the Driver is using to get the job done. Don't take it personally—unless, of course, you've done something to offend. Accept the fact that many people of this style are fairly impersonal in their manner of working.

Be Clear About Your Goals and Plans

Drivers are the most goal-oriented of the styles. They also take a more planned approach to their work than most people. The Amiable is more apt to take a fairly casual approach to goal setting and planning. This can become a point of tension between the two styles.

1. *Engage in goal setting.* A Driver expects you to have a very clear and specific understanding of what you are trying to achieve.

2. *Set stretch goals.* Don't think Drivers are content if you show them a set of run-of-the-mill goals and objectives. They expect you to raise your sights and commit to meaningful goals. At the same time, Drivers are realists. So set stretch goals that are achievable.

3. *Plan your work.* The Driver doesn't want you to waste time crafting ornate plans. Just come up with a simple, straightforward, results-oriented guide to action.

Say What You Think

Drivers tend to speak up and express themselves candidly and directly. Amiables are apt to keep their thoughts to themselves and speak somewhat tentatively and indirectly. Here's how you can bridge that behavioral gap.

1. *Speak up more often.* Initiate conversations more often. In conversations and meetings, express yourself frequently enough so that

there's a more balanced give-and-take. Drivers usually want to know where people stand. They would rather not have to try to interpret the meaning of your silence or have to pry thoughts out of you.

2. *Tell more; ask less.* Say "Here's what I think . . ." rather than "Do you think it would make sense to . . . ?" Say "Please do this" instead of "Could you do this?"

3. *Make statements that are definite rather than tentative.* Avoid words like *try, perhaps, maybe, possibly,* etc. Be specific. Don't say you'll complete a project "as soon as possible": Say it will be done "by twelve noon next Tuesday."

4. *Eliminate gestures that suggest you lack confidence in the point you are making.* Don't shrug your shoulders, hold your palms up, or use facial expressions that undercut what you are saying, imply help-lessness, or suggest the avoidance of responsibility.

5. *Voice your disagreements.* When Drivers disagree with you, they usually come right out and say so. They expect the same from you. Face conflict more openly, stating your opinions frankly but tactfully. At the same time, try to avoid situations where you and the Driver are battling from entrenched positions.

6. *Don't gloss over problems.* Beat bad news to the punch. Then give regular, brief, frank reports on your progress regarding the problem situation.

Cut to the Chase

Amiables are interested in some kinds of information that Drivers could care less about. These very time-conscious people may get very stressed if you talk about things they don't think they need to know.

1. *Concentrate on high-priority issues.* Drivers seldom want to be briefed on as many topics as an Amiable may want to discuss. For example, in weekly meetings with his reports, a Driver probably wants to hear only about exceptions from what is expected: problems, potential problems, and better-than-anticipated performance—not all the areas of a subordinate's responsibilities. Be very disciplined about reducing the number of topics you initiate in conversations with Drivers.

2. *Present the main points and skip all but the most essential details.* Drivers rarely feel they need anything more than an overview. They'll ask for more information if they want it.

3. *If in doubt, leave it out.* This guideline reiterates the previous two. It's worth repeating, though, because when you eliminate from

the conversation those things that Drivers may think are extraneous, you greatly reduce their stress and impatience.

Be Well Organized in Your Communication

When communicating with you, Drivers expect you to be well organized, brief, practical, and factual. As an Amiable, on the other hand, you tend to be more casual and informal when you talk. So, when presenting ideas or recommendations to Drivers, you make your case better when you incorporate the following behaviors.

1. *Be prepared.* Drivers expect you to make good use of their time. Don't wing it; think things through in advance. Anticipate questions you may be asked. Even for one-on-one meetings, it's often appropriate to create an agenda. Most of the suggestions below are enhanced by using more than your customary preparation.
2. *Have a well-organized presentation.* Explain your thoughts systematically. It often helps to present your ideas as a series of points arranged in logical order.
3. *When making recommendations, offer two options for the Driver to choose between.* Provide information that helps the Driver assess the probable outcome of each alternative.
4. *Focus on the results* of the action being discussed. Very early in the discussion of a course of action, describe the outcomes that could be achieved by the approaches you advocate. Then, factually demonstrate that the outcomes you project are both desirable and achievable.
5. *Emphasize that you are recommending pragmatic ways of doing things.* Demonstrate to these practical people that the options you present are very workable, no-frills ways of getting the results they want.
6. *Provide accurate factual evidence.* When talking with Drivers, it's rarely advisable to use someone's opinion or recommendation as evidence. Hard, accurate facts persuade these folks, so keep your presentation objective. Don't rely on sentiment or emotional appeals. As the detective on TV's *Dragnet* series used to say, "Just the facts . . . just the facts."

In your initial efforts to flex to Drivers, you'll probably find it helpful to review the portrait of the Driver style found in Chapter Six, pages 43–46.

Relating to Other Amiables

When people of the same style work together, they may be too similar! They lack important differences that occur when people of two or more styles collaborate. Some style-based differences can be useful at times in developing productive work relationships. Thus when relating to another Amiable, you may sometimes find it advantageous to temporarily use behaviors that are more characteristic of one of the other styles. For example, when two Amiables are working together, they may be more productive if one becomes more time-conscious and goal-oriented, calling attention to milestones and deadlines. Also, Amiables tend to create exceptionally harmonious working relationships. When two Amiables are collaborating, it's often helpful if one strongly asserts a different point of view when that's appropriate. Similarly, Amiables are so people-oriented that when they are engaged in a project, they may become less productive because of spending excessive time on people issues. Or, they may come up with a rather bland recommendation because of not wanting to rock the boat.

Therefore, in relating to another Amiable make sure you don't overuse style-based tendencies or use them when it's inappropriate to do so. Also, look for times to add some of the strengths more characteristic of the other styles by temporarily modifying some of your behavior.

Appendix II

For *Drivers* Only: How to Flex to Each Style

The purpose of Appendix II is to coach Drivers on specific things they can do to create more productive relationships with people of each style.

Most of the recommendations are about temporary behavioral changes that you can make for just a few minutes, before resuming your more comfortable style-based ways. However, we also mention a few options that have more long-term implications.

Since this appendix is a planning aid, don't try to read it straight through. Instead, find the section that applies to the style you want to flex to:

- Expressives, page 136
- Analyticals, page 142
- Amiables, page 147
- Other Drivers, page 153

Read that section to figure out what you can do to make it easier for persons of that style to work effectively with you. Later, when you want to improve your relationship with someone of a different style, read the section dealing with that style. By working your way through the Appendix on an as-needed basis, you'll soon read all the sections and strengthen important relationships in the process.

Flexing to Expressives

As a Driver, you have much in common with Expressives. You are similar on one of the two behavioral dimensions of style: Both of you are more assertive than most people. Consequently, Expressives tend to appreciate your energetic, fast-paced ways.

In flexing to an Expressive, your major challenge is to get in sync with some of his more responsive behaviors. You're able to create a more effective working relationship with an Expressive by *temporarily* using some of the following types of behavior, within each of which a number of specifics are mentioned. Do several, but not necessarily all, of the suggested specifics. You'll probably think of additional ways to work better with the particular person you have in mind.

Make Personal Contact

Expressives like to have personal contact with those they work with. It's important to them that they get to know you and that you get to know them personally. Drivers need to remind themselves to take the time and make the effort to establish personal contact with Expressives they work with.

1. *Don't seem aloof.* Expressives are apt to see the more reserved Drivers as aloof and distant. Without overdoing it, demonstrate more warmth in your words, your tone of voice, and your facial expression.
2. *Be more casual and informal than usual.* Expressives are inclined to informality. The more formal tendencies of a Driver may make you seem somewhat impersonal. Let your hair down a bit in this conversation.
3. *At the outset, touch base personally.* The Expressive is put off by an immediate plunge into the agenda. Take a few minutes to build rapport at the beginning of a conversation. Show Expressives that you're interested in them as people. Give them an opening to talk about themselves. For example, you can inquire about their personal interests or their opinions on a topic that's being widely discussed.
4. *Disclose something about yourself.* Expressives are the most talkative of the styles, so you may have to look for an opening to get in a word about yourself. You don't have to go on at length, but do let them get to know you better.
5. *Talk about what's going on with other people, too.* The gregarious Expressive is interested in knowing the latest about people he knows.
6. *Look for opportunities for conversations that are not task-related.* When a meeting ends, there may be a few minutes for the two of you to catch up on one another's life. The goal is to be appropriately though not excessively sociable.

Focus More on Feelings

Expressives are very much in touch with and disclosing of their feelings. Whatever those feelings are, they influence and sometimes even dominate the Expressive's decisions, actions, and responses to others. Since Drivers are much less emotive, getting in sync with an Expressive's feelings is a key to working effectively with her.

1. *Be aware of what the Expressive is feeling.* It's not that an Expressive's emotional cues are subtle; they'll probably come across loud and clear. But everyone has selective perception, and the Driver is likely to become engrossed in the *content* of the conversation and miss the emotional component even when it's quite obvious. Since Expressives' emotions have major impact on what they do, it's crucial to stay in touch with what they're feeling.
2. *Acknowledge the Expressive's feelings.* When Expressives are up about something they're working on, acknowledge the feelings: "You're excited about the way project X is going." When they're down, reflect those feelings, too: "You're frustrated that just when you got Sandy trained, she was transferred to another department and now you have to start breaking in a new rep."
3. *Don't overreact to the Expressive's highs and lows.* Expressives have greater mood swings than any of the styles. When they're high, they are energetic and excited about what they're doing. When they're low, they feel discouraged and unappreciated. As a Driver you are probably even-keeled in emotional terms. Don't read too much into the Expressive's extremes of feeling, unless they persist over time. An Expressive's feeling states are more fleeting than most people's; he'll probably be in a very different mood shortly.
4. *Show more feelings yourself.* If you are delighted about something, say so. If you disappointed, let that be known. When you are annoyed, talk about your feelings as well as what is bugging you. Say something like, "I'm irritated that you missed this deadline." Let your body language convey more of your feelings, too. For example, when expressing feelings, put more inflection in your voice.
5. *Demonstrate more enthusiasm.* When relating to an Expressive, showing enthusiasm is a particularly important way of disclosing more feeling. Though Expressives get dispirited at times, they are the most enthusiastic of the styles. When trying to sell an idea to an Expressive, your enthusiasm itself may be more persuasive than a logical presentation of the facts of the case. If you don't show excitement about the idea, the Expressive is apt to think you lack confidence in it. Also, whenever you're genuinely enthusiastic for the Expressive's projects and victories, share that feeling.
6. *Don't read too much into an Expressive's volatile verbal attacks.* Remember, under normal circumstances, people of this style are very emotive and more given to exaggeration than any of the styles.

When the Expressive is angry, emotions and exaggerations tend to become more pronounced. Try not to take the angry comments literally. The Expressive has more temper to control than most people, so don't assume that the derogatory things said in a fit of anger accurately communicate her thinking. However, if the verbal abuse becomes excessive, find a way to put an end to it.

Cooperate With the Expressive's Conversational Spontaneity

It's important to realize that when Expressives talk, they're often "thinking out loud." Expressives sometimes ask, "How will I know what I'm thinking unless I say it?" Above-the-line styles tend to get their ducks in order before they speak. If either you or the Expressive doesn't adapt to the style-based differences in verbal spontaneity, communication snafus are likely.

1. *Allow enough time for the conversation.* Although Expressives' speech is fast-paced, their tendency to tell stories and skip from one topic to another can be quite time-consuming, so don't impose tight time constraints on your meeting with an Expressive.
2. *Keep a balance between flowing with an Expressive's digressions and getting back on track.* With Expressives you can expect to have long, wandering conversations. If you try to keep these highly assertive people from getting sidetracked onto other subjects, you're apt to end in an unproductive power struggle. However, after they've digressed for a while, you sometimes need to tactfully get the conversation refocused.
3. *Spend time in mutual exploration.* Once Expressives are sold on an idea, they may not want to explore other options. Similarly, Drivers are likely to have their own point of view. When two highly assertive people argue from fixed positions, the result can be an unproductive "dialogue of the deaf." To avoid this, listen carefully to the Expressive's ideas and converse in such a way that there's a mutual discussion of the problem and possible solutions.
4. *Be patient with overstatements.* With their tendency to be dramatic, Expressives are liable to exaggerate to make a point. Unless a more accurate understanding of a particular matter is essential to the discussion, don't press for accuracy. Concentrate instead on the idea the Expressive is trying to get across, and let the conversation move on.
5. *Be tactful in responding to contradictions in what the Expressive says.* Since Expressives are thinking things through while they talk, they may make contradictory statements in the same conversation without realizing it. If the conflicting thoughts are not germane to

what's being discussed, just overlook the discrepancy. If it's central to what is being talked about, find a diplomatic way to get at the actual meaning of the Expressive's statements.

Be Open to the Expressive's Fun-Loving Side

Expressives are the most playful and fun-loving of the styles. They like to mix pleasure with business. If you lighten up a little when working with an Expressive, you may be able to get more done than if you stick strictly to business.

1. *Don't get impatient if the Expressive indulges in a few jokes.* When you are ready to get down to business, an Expressive is apt to regale you with jokes. Instead of getting upset at what might seem like a waste of time, relax and enjoy the humor. However, there's no need for you to get into the act with jokes of your own unless you choose to.
2. *Be relaxed about a certain amount of fooling around.* Even in the midst of serious business, an Expressive may engage in horseplay. Go with the flow for a while. It may be the release that the Expressive needs before focusing again on the business at hand.
3. *Try to create a more pleasant atmosphere for your conversation.* Sitting behind a table in a sterile conference room or talking across a desk in someone's office is not the Expressive's cup of tea. If the weather and location permit, talk while taking a noontime stroll, or over breakfast or lunch at a favorite bistro. . . . Put your mind to it, and you'll find more options than you expect.

Give the Expressive Recognition

Expressives, even more than most people, like recognition.

1. *Show appreciation for the Expressive's contribution.* Expressives thrive on sincere compliments. For the Expressive, it's even better if the appreciation is expressed publicly.
2. *Let the Expressive be in the spotlight.* By and large, people of this style find it easy to be the center of attention. Try to find ways for them to get the recognition they enjoy while making sure everyone on a project gets the credit they deserve.

Communicate on the Expressive's Wavelength

When speaking with an Expressive, realize that information you find convincing may carry little weight with the Expressive. Here are some ways to communicate on the Expressive's wavelength.

1. *Summarize face-to-face communication in writing.* Expressives like to talk things over face-to-face. If that's not possible, try using the telephone. When you reach a definite conclusion in your face-to-face meeting or phone call, paraphrase it. Then, when the issue is important, follow up immediately with a *brief* written summary of what was decided.

2. *Try to support the Expressive's vision.* People of this style are dreamers—in both the best and the worst senses of the word. They often have a vision of a better future for their department or organization. But their vision may be unrealistic or poorly aligned with the direction of the corporation. When you can, help Expressives inject realism into their proposed ventures. And on those occasions when you can't conscientiously support their visionary proposals, be respectful as well as clear in expressing your opposition.

3. *Steer clear of the nitty-gritty.* Mention even fewer details than you normally would. When Expressives want to know more, they'll ask. However, when details are of crucial importance, make sure they are not glossed over.

4. *Don't overdo facts and logic.* What seems like a desirable amount of facts and logic to a Driver undoubtedly seems like overkill to an Expressive. Edit out of your conversation any facts or logic that aren't absolutely essential to making your point.

5. *Highlight recommendations of others*—especially recommendations of people the Expressive knows or respects. The testimony of a friend or of people who have successfully used the same approach probably carries more weight than tables of statistics or other impersonal evidence.

6. *Demonstrate concern about the human side.* When possible, invite the Expressive's input before a decision is made. Discuss the effect on people of new policies, procedures, processes, and projects. For example, when discussing a new practice, in addition to pointing out its cost-cutting advantages, be sure to add a comment such as, "Most people will like the way it cuts down on the excessive overtime they've been complaining about."

7. *Recommend a particular course of action.* Rather than present Expressives with options, it's often best to help them get enthused about what you think is the best alternative.

8. *Provide incentives when possible.* Everybody likes an incentive, but few people are as motivated by them as Expressives.

Provide Considerable Freedom

Like Drivers, Expressives want to do things their own way. These free spirits want to avoid as many restraints as they can.

1. *Help Expressives put their personal stamp on what they do.* They want their work to be a form of self-expression. Regarding the things they are involved with, they want to be able to say, "I did it my way." However, Drivers are sometimes very insistent about how they want things done. When possible, avoid pressuring the Expressive into doing things your way.

2. *Empower Expressives to do new things.* They hate doing the same old things in the same old ways. Look for ways to help them inject some novelty into their work. Also, try to find new approaches to the way the two of you work together.

3. *Be willing to improvise when you can.* You are probably much more organized than your Expressive colleague. You may be used to planning your work and working your plan. However, for the Expressive, planning is a drag and following a plan feels like being put in a straitjacket. Be open to the possibility of winging it from time to time.

4. *Cater to their physical restlessness.* Expressives hate to sit still even more than you do. Don't just sit and talk with an Expressive for long periods; create reasons to get up and move around a bit. Also, since Expressives don't like the confinement of a desk-type job, when it's in your power help them find projects or roles that enable them to release some of their physical energy.

5. *Avoid power struggles.* The Expressive is more assertive than most people. You are too. Because of that, the two of you have much in common. However, when two such assertive people work together, there's always the danger that sparks will fly. If that begins to happen, temporarily find ways of being less assertive. Listen more, and listen better (pages 143–144). Decrease your vocal intensity, phrase your ideas more provisionally, and be more negotiable (page 144).

In your initial efforts to flex to Expressives, you'll probably find it helpful to review the portrait of the Expressive style found in Chapter Six, pages 38–43.

Flexing to Analyticals

As a Driver you have much in common with Analyticals. You are similar on one of the two basic dimensions of style: Both of you are less responsive than most people. Consequently, Analyticals generally appreciate your focus on task and your objective approach to things.

In flexing to Analyticals, your major challenge is to get in sync with some of their less assertive behaviors. You should be able to create a more effective working relationship with an Analytical by temporarily using some of the following four types of behavior, within each which a number of specifics are mentioned. Do several, but not necessarily all, of the specifics within the types of behavior you plan to emphasize. You'll probably think of additional ways to work better with the specific Analytical you have in mind.

Slow Your Pace

Analyticals walk slowly, talk slowly, decide slowly. To fast-paced Drivers, it seems they do everything at a snail's pace. But to the Analytical, the fast pace of a typical Driver is very uncomfortable. It throws Analyticals off their stride. If you want to work better with those thorough and deliberate people, slow down and get more in sync with their natural rhythm.

1. *Talk slower.* When Drivers talk at their natural pace, Analyticals often have to strain to keep up. Why put yourself at that disadvantage when making a point?
2. *Don't create unnecessarily tight deadlines.* Few Drivers understand how very stressful it can be for Analyticals to do things at a rate that would be only mildly uncomfortable for the Driver. Then, too, as the Analytical knows full well, there are many times when haste merely makes waste.
3. *When it comes to making decisions, don't rush the Analytical unnecessarily.* Realize that your style and the Analytical's are very different when it comes to making decisions. Compared to most people, you make choices quickly and easily. For the Analytical, decision making is a slow, more difficult, and more stressful process. If you add a time crunch to the scenario, the Analytical's stress may go even higher. There are times when these slow deciders need a nudge. But if time is not of the essence, let them make decisions in their own way: deliberately.
4. *Take time to be more thorough.* Analyticals like to do things slowly and thoroughly. When working with Analyticals especially, look for situations where you can increase your productivity as well as rapport by taking a more thorough approach than you normally would.

Listen More, Listen Better

Drivers tend to speak their minds; Analyticals are apt to keep their opinions to themselves. If the Driver is also a poor listener, which is often the case, the Analytical is apt to clam up even more. It's hard to have a productive work relationship when one person isn't talking. Drivers don't get the information they need, and the Analytical's active participation begins to dry up. A growing rift settles into the relationship. Though the conversational lopsidedness is certainly not all your fault, it is in your best interest to improve the situation by listening more and better.

1. *Talk less.* When you are with an Analytical who tends to be on the quiet side, make a disciplined effort to talk less. Because the amount of talking you do is habitual, you probably find that it's not easy to decrease it. Drivers who commit to having balanced conversations with Analyticals are usually helped by the method described in Chapter Eleven, "Antidote to Domineering: Listen Better and Speak Provisionally," pages 89–91.
2. *Provide more and longer pauses to make it easier for the Analytical to get into the conversation.* Analyticals need longer pauses than Drivers, so give them longer and more frequent pauses.
3. *Invite Analyticals to speak.* Request their input on the agenda; ask their opinions on the topics you cover. When explaining your thoughts, draw them into the conversation with checking questions: "How does this fit with your thinking?" "I'm interested in your point of view on what I've said." "How does this sound to you?"
4. *Reflect back to the speaker the gist of what you hear.* This is a way of acknowledging a person's viewpoint without either agreeing or disagreeing with it. Once you've reflected back what the person has said, pause to see if she wishes to add anything. Then it's your turn to give your response. Begin by stating points of agreement. Choose your words carefully if you disagree with parts of what the Analytical said. If people of this style think they'll get clobbered when they do speak up, you'll hear even less from them in the future.
5. *Don't interrupt.* When you cut off another person in midsentence to add more comments of your own, it's not unreasonable for him to assume you don't value his opinion. That can be a real barrier to constructive work relationships.
6. *Don't finish the other person's sentences.* It can try the patience of a fast-paced Driver to listen to the hesitant speech of a particularly slow-talking Analytical. But patience is exactly what's required for a Driver to flex effectively to an Analytical.

Don't Come on Too Strong

Analyticals, by definition, are less assertive than you. Their body language isn't as forceful. They don't speak as often, and when they do, they're not as emphatic. So when you use your normal Driver behavior, the mismatch in assertiveness may lead the Analytical to think of you as pushy. A work relationship certainly isn't enhanced when one person feels he is being pushed around by another. Also, if your way of communicating makes you seem dogmatic, the Analytical may become even more silent than usual, thus depriving you of important information. Here are some things you can do to avoid coming on too strong to Analyticals.

1. *Decrease the intensity of your eye contact.* When speaking to an Analytical, look away a bit more than you normally would. When you do make eye contact, soften your gaze somewhat.
2. *Don't gesture too emphatically.* Drivers often develop some forceful gestures, such as pointing a finger, to underscore a point. This type of gesture tends to be a bit much for most people: It's certainly to be avoided when you are talking to an Analytical.
3. *Decrease your vocal intensity.* Your voice is probably louder than the Analytical's, so you may want to drop the volume a few decibels. Beyond volume, however, Drivers often have an insistent sound to their voice. Once you become aware of your vocal characteristics, you can learn how to sound more casual but still be influential.
4. *Lean back when you make a point.* Do as Analyticals do and lean back when you're talking. Fortunately, when you assume a more laid-back posture, you probably show less intensity in your eye contact, gestures, and voice.
5. *Phrase your ideas more provisionally.* Analyticals often choose language that's quite tentative. Drivers, on the other hand, often select words that suggest a more dogmatic stance than they may mean to take. When you use this kind of phrasing with fairly insistent body language, it may sound as if you are trying to rule out any further discussion. These are some phrases that can help you come across in a less dogmatic manner: "Here's an idea off the top of my head." "I'd like to run this up the flagpole." "I like that idea. What if we also . . . " When you don't agree with something, you can take an approach like this: "I'd like to play devil's advocate for a few minutes."
6. *Be more negotiable.* When possible, avoid imposing your solution to a problem on your Analytical co-worker; that's a win-lose approach. A series of win-lose struggles undermines the relationship. Instead, through a win-win style of negotiation or cooperative problem solving, jointly create solutions to the problems you encounter.

Communicate on the Analytical's Wavelength

As with each style, Analyticals have their own preferences about how they'd like things presented to them. If you have an idea you want to get across or a recommendation you wish to make, consider incorporating the following behaviors.

1. *Be prepared.* Analyticals expect you to be well prepared. Dig up all the data they may want. Anticipate questions you may be asked. Even for one-on-one meetings, it's often appropriate to create an agenda. Consider getting the agenda to the Analytical in advance; she may want to think about the topics beforehand. Most of the suggestions below are enhanced by using more than your customary preparation.

2. *Go into great detail.* Analyticals want to delve into the particulars; they thrive on specifics. They want to make sure all the ground has been covered before they make a decision. You gain credibility with people of this style when they see that you've chased down every detail.

3. *Give a sound rationale for narrowing the options.* Analyticals want to consider all the alternatives. While this tendency often helps them make good decisions, it also increases their tendency to be inordinately indecisive. You can help them weed out some of the weaker alternatives by giving them logical and factual reasons for doing so.

4. *Mention the problems and disadvantages of the proposal you put forward.* In addition to mentioning the pluses of your recommendation, tell the Analytical about the downside, too. She undoubtedly respects you for doing so. Then, build your credibility further by recommending ways of dealing with the problems and disadvantages.

5. *Show why the approach you advocate is best.* For Analyticals, "best" is a combination of quality, economy, and low risk. You have to figure out the relative weight of each of these criteria for a particular Analytical in a particular set of circumstances. "Best" for this style includes *long-term benefits* as well as immediate advantages. Discuss the future in terms of probabilities: "Here's a projection of what's likely to happen. . . . " Since the Analytical is conservative when it comes to risk, if possible show why your approach is a fairly safe bet.

6. *Be accurate.* People of this style are both precise and skeptical. They abhor a superficial gathering of information or careless reporting of it. Where others might settle for approximations, Analyticals

want meticulously correct information. So be painstakingly accurate in what you report to people of this style.

7. *Provide written support materials, and/or follow up in writing.* Analyticals tend to prefer the written word to the spoken. Even so, it's
best to make an oral presentation as well. That way you can note
the Analytical's reactions and answer questions. At the same time,
cater to the Analytical's preference for written communication by
preparing well-thought-out support materials and/or a follow-up
report. You may want to include a step-by-step timetable for implementing any decisions.

8. *Be prepared to listen to more than you want to know.* When Analyticals
talk, they often present far more information than most people
think is necessary. They explain their ideas or discuss progress on
projects in what may feel to you like overwhelming detail. This
much minutiae may be boring and difficult to follow. Be patient
and stay tuned in; Analyticals appreciate your attentiveness. And,
there's probably information you need to know buried somewhere in all that detail.

*In your initial efforts to flex to Analyticals, you'll probably find it helpful
to review the portrait of the Analytical style found in Chapter Six, pages 30–33.*

Flexing to Amiables

As a Driver, you differ from the Amiable on both of the basic dimensions
of style. The Amiable is less assertive and less responsive than you are.
So you are likely to experience more style-based differences with Amiables than with either Analyticals or Expressives, both of whom have one
basic dimension of behavior in common with you. As a result there are
more types of behavior that you can modify when flexing to an Amiable
than when flexing to any other style.

As you read the types of *temporary* adjustment of behavior that can
help you get in sync with Amiables, select carefully the one to four types
you think will help you work best with a particular Amiable. It's not easy
to change habitual behavior, even for a short time, so be sure to select only
one to four types of behavior to work on. Within each type or category
of behavior, a number of specifics are mentioned. Do several, but not
necessarily all, of the specifics within the behavioral category you plan to
emphasize. You'll probably think of additional ways to work better with
the specific Amiable you have in mind.

Make Genuine Personal Contact

The Amiable wants to be treated as a human being and not as a function
or a role only. The Driver, who is more task-oriented than most people,

may need to remember to show a sincere interest in the Amiable as a person.

1. *Don't seem aloof.* Be more casual and informal than usual. Without overdoing it, demonstrate more warmth in your words, your tone of voice, and your facial expression.
2. *At the outset, touch base personally.* Amiables are usually uncomfortable with a cold, headlong plunge into the agenda. At the beginning of a conversation, take a few minutes to build rapport. Show that you are interested in the Amiable as a person. Give Amiables an opening to talk about themselves.
3. *Disclose something about yourself.* The Amiable likes to invite you to talk about yourself. Don't brush it off with, "Oh, things are fine." Briefly, let him know some things that are going on in your life.
4. *Make the most of opportunities for conversations that are not task-related.* For example, when waiting for a meeting to begin, don't read a report; use that time to chat with Amiables and others who like more personal contact. When a meeting concludes, you can also create opportunities for social interchange. You'll find many other occasions when you can be in touch with Amiables as people. The goal is to be appropriately though not excessively sociable.

Slow Your Pace

Amiables walk slowly, talk slowly, decide slowly. To fast-paced Drivers, it seems like they do everything at a crawl. But to the Amiable, the fast pace of a typical Driver is very uncomfortable. It throws Amiables off their stride. If you want to work better with Amiables, slow down and get more in sync with their natural rhythm.

1. *Talk slower.* When Drivers talk at their natural pace, Amiables often have to strain to keep up. Why put yourself at that disadvantage when making a point?
2. *Don't create unnecessarily tight deadlines.* Remember, it can be very stressful for the Amiable to do things at your pace.
3. *When it comes to decision making, don't rush the Amiable unnecessarily.* There are times when these slow deciders need a nudge. But unless time is of the essence, let them make decisions on their own schedule.

Listen More, Listen Better

Drivers tend to speak their minds; Amiables are apt to keep their opinions to themselves. If the Driver is also a poor listener, which is often the case, the Amiable is apt to clam up even more. It's hard to have a productive work relationship when one person isn't talking. Drivers don't get the information they need, and the Amiable's active participation begins to dry up. A rift appears in the relationship. Although the conversational lopsidedness is certainly not all your fault, it's certainly in your best interest to improve the situation by listening more and better.

1. *Talk less.* When you are with an Amiable who tends to be on the quiet side, make a disciplined effort to talk less. It's not easy. Drivers who commit to having balanced conversations with Amiables are usually helped by the method described in Chapter Eleven, "Antidote to Domineering: Listen Better and Speak Provisionally," pages 89–91.
2. *Provide more and longer pauses to make it easier for the Amiable to get into the conversation.* Amiables need longer pauses than Drivers, so give them longer and more frequent pauses.
3. *Invite Amiables to speak.* Request their input on the agenda. Ask their opinion on the topics you cover. When explaining your thoughts, draw them into the conversation with checking questions: "How does this fit with your thinking?" "I'm interested in your point of view on what I've said." "How does this sound to you?"
4. *Reflect back to the speaker the gist of what you hear.* This is a way of acknowledging a person's viewpoint without either agreeing or disagreeing. Once you've reflected back what the person has said, pause to see if he wishes to add anything. Then it's your turn to give your response. Begin by stating points of agreement. If you disagree with something, choose your words carefully. If people of this style think they'll get clobbered when they speak up, you'll hear even less from them in the future.
5. *Don't interrupt.* When you cut off another person in midsentence in order to add more comments of your own, it's not unreasonable for her to assume you don't value her opinion. That can be a real barrier to constructive work relationships.
6. *Don't finish Amiables' sentences.* It can try the patience of a fast-paced Driver to listen to the hesitant speech of a particularly slow-talking Amiable. But patience is exactly what's required for a Driver who wants to flex effectively to an Amiable.

Don't Come on Too Strong

Amiables, by definition, are less assertive than you. Their body language isn't as forceful. They don't speak as often, and when they do they're not as emphatic. So when you use your normal Driver behavior, the mismatch in assertiveness may lead the Amiable to think of you as pushy. A work relationship certainly isn't enhanced when one person feels pushed around by another. Also, if your way of communicating makes you seem dogmatic, the Amiable may become even more silent than usual, thus depriving you of important information. Here are some things you can do to avoid coming on too strong to Amiables.

1. *Decrease the intensity of your eye contact.* The Driver's eye contact is more intense than the Amiable's. When speaking to an Amiable, soften your gaze.
2. *Don't gesture too emphatically.* Drivers often develop some forceful gestures, such as pointing a finger, to underscore a point. This type of gesture tends to be somewhat disturbing for most people: It's certainly to be avoided when you are talking with an Amiable.
3. *Decrease your vocal intensity.* Drop the volume a few decibels. Try to sound less insistent. Once you become aware of your vocal characteristics, you can learn how to sound more casual and still be influential.
4. *Lean back when you make a point.* Do as they do and lean back when you're talking. Fortunately, when you assume a more laid-back posture, you probably show less intensity in your eye contact, gestures, and voice.
5. *Phrase your ideas more provisionally.* Amiables often choose language that's quite tentative. Drivers, on the other hand, often select words that suggest a more dogmatic stance than they mean to take. When this kind of phrasing is coupled with a fairly insistent body language, it may sound as if you are trying to rule out any discussion. These are some phrases that can help you come across in a less dogmatic way: "Here's an idea off the top of my head." "I'd like to run this up the flagpole." "I like that idea. What if we also . . . " When you don't agree with something, you can take an approach like this: "I'd like to play devil's advocate for a few minutes."
6. *Be more negotiable.* When possible, avoid imposing your solution to a problem on your Amiable co-worker, for that's a win-lose approach. A series of win-lose struggles undermines the relationship. Instead, through a win-win approach to negotiation or cooperative problem solving, jointly create solutions to the problems you encounter.

Focus More on Feelings

Amiables are expressive of their emotions and sensitive to the feelings of others. You can get more in sync with Amiables by focusing more on feelings—both theirs and your own.

1. *Look at the person you are conversing with* so you can take in body-language cues.
2. *Concentrate on the meaning of the person's body language.* Drivers are apt to give excessive attention to the words that are spoken and overlook important nonverbal cues. As you notice the nonverbal signals, keep asking yourself, "What does this suggest about this person's feelings right now?"
3. *Note how the other person reacts.* Amiables dislike conflict and may not verbalize their disagreement or dissatisfaction. Changes in their body language can tip you off as to how they may be reacting to what is being said. Once you surmise that the other person has negative feelings about a proposal, you can invite his or her reaction: "Some people are leery of this part of the plan. I'm interested in your thoughts about it."
4. *Demonstrate more feelings yourself.* If you are pleased about something, say so. If you are disappointed, let that be known. Let your body language express your feelings more. Put a little more inflection into your voice. Smile a bit more to demonstrate warmth toward the person you are with.

Be Supportive

Amiables are supportive, and they expect others to be supportive in turn. They feel that's the least one human being should be able to expect from another.

1. *Listen empathically so the Amiable feels heard and understood.* Truly listening to someone is one of the most supportive things we can do for that person. Earlier, we emphasized the importance of listening, but it's so important for Drivers flexing to Amiables that it bears repeating.
2. *Express sincere appreciation for the Amiable's contributions.* A number of behavioral scientists say it's desirable to "stroke" a person five times as much as you criticize or give negative feedback. Even more than most people, Amiables thrive on appreciation. Find lots of ways to say, "Thanks for your good work." Also, decrease the number of critical and judgmental statements you make. When you do give criticism, make sure it's constructive.
3. *Lend a helping hand.* Amiables are the most helpful of the styles. They often drop what they're doing to aid someone who's in a pinch. They appreciate it when you spot an opportunity to give them a hand when they're under pressure.

Provide Structure

Amiables tend to be most comfortable and work best in stable, clearly structured situations. Do what you can to contribute to that stability and structure without being overly constraining.

1. When it's within your area of responsibility, *make sure the Amiable's job is well defined and goals are clearly established.* Amiables work best when their roles are clarified and their goals are set.
2. *Help the Amiable plan difficult projects and design complex work processes.* Planning is not the Amiable's forte. When you help an Amiable develop a sound plan or design an effective work process, he usually takes it from there.
3. *Reduce uncertainty.* Amiables are not likely to function well in highly ambiguous situations. Try not to put the Amiable in an unstable, rapidly fluctuating situation.
4. *Demonstrate loyalty.* In most cases Amiables feel a greater-than-average loyalty to the people they work with and the organizations they work in. Consequently, they expect you to demonstrate your loyalty to them, their co-workers and the organization. Amiables will probably be turned off if they hear you take potshots at employees or the organization. Instead of voicing criticisms, make constructive suggestions for improvement, and make them directly to the people involved.

Demonstrate Interest in the Human Side

Amiables tend to take a people-oriented approach whereas Drivers are prone to be task-oriented. When working with an Amiable, give increased attention to the human side of things.

1. *Invite Amiables' input on matters that affect them.* Although they aren't as demanding as most people, they like to be consulted on matters pertaining to them.
2. *Show that other people support the idea you are advancing.* This people-oriented style is often influenced more by the experiences and opinions of others than by cold facts. Let them know about the positive feelings others in the organization have about your proposal. Provide evidence from experts. Mention testimonies of others who have successfully used a similar approach. If, in the process, the Amiable discovers that there's little risk to the recommended course of action, so much the better.
3. *Discuss the effects of decisions on people and their morale.* Be alert to and speak about the effects on people of new policies, procedures,

processes, and projects. For example, when discussing a new practice, in addition to pointing out its cost-cutting advantages be sure
to add something like, "Most people will like the way it cuts down
on the excessive overtime they've been complaining about."

4. When appropriate, *provide an opportunity for the Amiable to talk with
others* before committing to a decision.

*In your initial efforts to flex to Amiables, you'll probably find it helpful to
review the portrait of the Amiable style found in Chapter Six, pages 33–38.*

Relating to Other Drivers

When people of the same style work together, they may be too similar!
They lack important differences that occur when people of two or more
styles collaborate. Some of these style-based differences can be useful at
times in developing productive work relationships. Thus when relating
to another Driver, you sometimes find it advantageous to temporarily use
behaviors that are more characteristic of one of the other styles. For example, Drivers are often overly decisive. When a couple of Drivers are working together, they may be more productive if one of them suggests further
exploration before making a decision. Also, Drivers tend to be exceptionally independent. When two Drivers are collaborating, it's often helpful
if one encourages interdependency by checking out what others think.
One of the two Drivers could help them both focus more on long-term
impact rather than solely on short-term goals. Similarly, Drivers are so
task-oriented that when two of them are engaged in a project, they may
become less productive over time because neither one puts in the effort
required to maintain a good working relationship. Or, they may come up
with an otherwise brilliant recommendation that ultimately fails because
they paid scant attention to the human side of the change they implemented.

Therefore, in relating to another Driver, make sure you don't overuse
style-based tendencies or use them when it's inappropriate to do so. Also,
look for times to add some of the strengths more characteristic of the
other styles by temporarily modifying some of your behavior.

When two highly assertive Drivers work together, there's always a
danger that they'll end up in a power struggle. This is the biggest threat
to Driver-Driver relationships. If you find that you and another Driver
are beginning to butt heads together, temporarily find ways of being less
assertive. Listen more and listen better. Decrease your vocal intensity,
phrase your ideas more provisionally, and be more negotiable.

Appendix III

For *Expressives* Only: How to Flex to Each Style

The purpose of Appendix III is to coach Expressives on specific things they can do to create more productive relationships with people of each style.

Most of the recommendations are about temporary behavioral changes that you can make for a few minutes, before resuming your more comfortable style-based ways. However, we also mention a few options that have more long-term implications.

Since this appendix is a planning aid, don't try to read it straight through. Instead, find the section that applies to the style you want to flex to:

- Amiables, page 154
- Drivers, page 158
- Analyticals, page 161
- Other Expressives, page 168

Read that section to figure out what you can do to make it easier for the people of that style to work effectively with you. Later, when you want to improve your relationship with someone of a different style, read the section dealing with that style. By working your way through the Appendix on an as-needed basis, you'll soon read all the sections and strengthen important relationships in the process.

Flexing to Amiables

As an Expressive, you have much in common with Amiables. You are similar on one of the two behavioral dimensions of style: Both of you are more responsive than most people. Consequently, Amiables tend to appreciate your warmth, your friendliness, and your focus on people.

In flexing to an Amiable, your major challenge is to get in sync with some of her less assertive behaviors. You create a more effective working relationship with an Amiable by *temporarily* using some of the following types of behavior, within each of which a number of specifics are mentioned. Do several, but not necessarily all, of the suggested specifics. You'll probably think of additional ways to work better with the particular person you have in mind.

Slow Your Pace

To the Amiable, the fast pace of a typical Expressive is very uncomfortable. It throws Amiables off their stride. If you want to work better with Amiables, slow down and get more in sync with their natural rhythm.

1. *Talk slower.* Many Expressives talk a lot faster than Amiables. When Expressives talk at their natural pace, Amiables often have to strain to keep up. This is certainly not a user-friendly way of speaking with people. Why put yourself at that disadvantage when making a point?
2. *Don't create unnecessarily tight deadlines.* Remember, it can be very stressful for the Amiable to do things at your pace.
3. *When it comes to decision making, don't rush the Amiable unnecessarily.* There are times when these slow deciders need a nudge. But unless time is of the essence, let them make decisions on their own schedule.

Listen More, Listen Better

Expressives tend to speak their minds; Amiables are apt to keep their opinions to themselves. If the Expressive is also a poor listener, which is often the case, the Amiable is apt to clam up even more. It's hard to have a productive work relationship when one person is doing most of the talking. The Amiable's active participation begins to dry up, and the Expressive doesn't get the needed information. There's probably a growing rift in the relationship. Although the conversational lopsidedness is certainly not all your fault, it's definitely in your best interest to improve the situation by listening more and better.

1. *Talk less.* When you are with an Amiable who tends to be on the quiet side, make a disciplined effort to talk less. Expressives who commit to having balanced conversations with Amiables are usually helped by the method described in Chapter Eleven, "Antidote

to Domineering: Listen Better and Speak Provisionally," pages 89–91. Although the section in Chapter Eleven was written for Drivers, the method is equally useful for Expressives.

2. *Provide more and longer pauses to make it easier for the Amiable to get into the conversation.* Amiables need longer pauses than Expressives. So give them long and more frequent pauses.

3. *Invite Amiables to speak.* Request their input on the agenda; ask their opinion on the topics you cover. When explaining your thoughts, draw them into the conversation with checking questions: "How does this fit with your thinking?" "I'm interested in your point of view on what I've said." "How does this sound to you?"

4. *Reflect back to the speaker the gist of what you hear.* This is a way of acknowledging a person's viewpoint without either agreeing or disagreeing with it. Once you've reflected back what the person has said, pause to see if he wishes to add anything. Then it's your turn to give your response. Begin by stating points of agreement. When you disagree, choose your words carefully. If people of this style think they'll get clobbered when they speak up, you'll hear even less from them in the future.

5. *Don't interrupt.* When you cut off another person in midsentence to add more comments of your own, it's not unreasonable for that person to assume you don't value her opinion. That can be a real barrier to constructive work relationships.

6. *Don't finish other people's sentences.* It can try the patience of a fast-paced Expressive to listen to the hesitant speech of a particularly slow-talking Amiable. But patience is a prime requisite for an Expressive who wants to flex effectively to an Amiable.

Don't Come on Too Strong

Amiables, by definition, are less assertive than you. Their body language isn't as forceful. They don't speak as often, and when they do they're not as emphatic. So when you use your normal Expressive behavior, the mismatch in assertiveness may lead the Amiable to think of you as pushy. A work relationship certainly isn't enhanced when one person feels he is being pushed around by another. Also, if your way of communicating makes you seem dogmatic, the Amiable may become even more silent than usual, thus depriving you of important information. Here are some things you can do to avoid coming on too strong to Amiables.

1. *Decrease the intensity of your eye contact.* The Expressive's eye contact is more intense and constant than the Amiable's. When speaking to an Amiable, soften your gaze somewhat.

2. *Restrain your gestures.* Both Expressives and Amiables tend to talk with their hands. However, the Amiable's gestures are much smaller and less dramatic. When talking with Amiables, don't gesture as emphatically as you may be inclined to.

3. *Decrease your vocal intensity.* As a group, Expressives have louder voices than any of the styles. Soft-spoken Amiables find it irritating when someone speaks to them in a loud voice during a normal conversation. You get through to this style much more effectively when you lower your voice.

4. *Lean back when you make a point.* Do as they do and lean back when you're talking. Fortunately, when you assume a more laid-back posture, you show less intensity in your eye contact, gestures, and voice.

5. *Phrase your ideas more provisionally.* Amiables often choose language that's quite tentative. Expressives, on the other hand, often select words that suggest a more dogmatic stance than they mean to take. This kind of phrasing coupled with fairly insistent body language may sound as if you are trying to rule out any discussion. These are some phrases that can help you come across in a less dogmatic way: "Here's an idea off the top of my head." "I'd like to run this up the flagpole." "I like that idea. What if we also . . ." When you don't agree with something, you can take an approach like this: "I'd like to play devil's advocate for a few minutes."

6. *Be more negotiable.* When possible, avoid imposing your solution to a problem on your Amiable co-worker. Instead, through a win-win approach to negotiation or cooperative problem solving, jointly create solutions to the problems you encounter.

Be Supportive

Amiables are supportive of other people, and they expect others to be supportive in turn. They feel that's the least one human being should expect from another.

1. *Listen empathically so the Amiable feels heard and understood.* Truly listening to others is one of the most supportive things we can do for them. Although we mentioned the importance of listening earlier, it is so important for Expressives flexing to Amiables that it bears repeating.

2. *Express sincere appreciation for the Amiable's contributions.* Amiables thrive on appreciation. Find lots of ways to say, "Thanks for your good work." Also, decrease the number of critical and judgmental

statements you make. When you do give criticism, make sure it's constructive.
3. *Lend a helping hand.* Amiables are the most helpful of the styles. They're apt to drop what they're doing to aid someone who's in a pinch. They appreciate it if you spot an opportunity to give them a hand when they're under pressure.

In your initial efforts to flex to Amiables, you'll probably find it helpful to review the portrait of the Amiable style found in Chapter Six, pages 33–38.

Flexing to Drivers

As an Expressive, you have much in common with Drivers. You are similar on one of the two behavioral dimensions of style: Both of you are more assertive than most people. Consequently, Drivers tend to appreciate your energetic, fast-paced ways.

In flexing to a Driver, your major challenge is to get in sync with some of his less responsive behaviors. You create a more effective working relationship with a Driver by temporarily using some of the following four types of behavior, within each of which a number of specifics are mentioned. Do several, but not necessarily all, of the suggested specifics. You'll probably think of additional ways to work better with the particular Driver you have in mind.

Be More Task-Oriented

The Driver is usually more task-oriented and the Expressive tends to be more people-oriented. When working with a Driver, you may want to give increased attention to the task side of things.

1. *Be on time.* Expressives are by far the least punctual of the styles—very annoying to most Drivers. When you're working with Drivers, watch your clock (and your calendar!) and be on time.
2. *Be a bit more formal.* Drivers tend toward the conservative in their clothing and grooming. You may want to have a somewhat conservative appearance when working with above-the-line styles. Also, don't be too flip or offbeat in your interactions with Drivers. It's best to take a businesslike approach to your interactions with Drivers—at least until they indicate a preference for a more informal relationship.
3. *Get right to business.* Don't give the impression that you're there to chat. But don't lose your human touch either. Limit the small talk. It's usually appropriate to spend a little time on openers, but keep

it brief and don't make it too personal. Then get right into what you're there to talk about.

4. *Stick to business.* Drivers are the most time-conscious of the styles. And they're not as people-oriented as the below-the-line styles. So they like to keep conversations and meetings short and to the point. The shorter the better. Even in a one-on-one meeting with a Driver, have an agenda and follow it. Don't digress. As you discuss the business at hand and are reminded of things that are tangential to the discussion, don't pursue them. The guideline is, "If in doubt, leave it out." When the time is up, depart quickly yet graciously.

Deemphasize Feelings

Drivers are less emotionally aware and less disclosing of their feelings than most people. Expressives, on the other hand, are more disclosing of their emotions than any style. You can get more in sync with Drivers by being less emotionally disclosing. Be more reserved, without becoming cold or aloof.

1. *Limit your facial expressiveness.* Match your facial expression more closely to your co-worker's seriousness.
2. *Limit your gestures.* The more reserved Driver may be distracted or even a bit disconcerted if you constantly talk with your hands. So, when working with Drivers, tone down the body English a little.
3. *Avoid touch.* Below-the-line people, especially many Expressives, spontaneously reach out and touch the person they're talking to. Above-the-line people, like Drivers, typically feel uneasy when someone touches them. Honor their preferences and avoid touch.
4. *Talk about what you think rather than about what you feel.* Think longer and harder about issues you're discussing with a Driver. The words you use are important, too. Saying "I *think* . . ." instead of "I feel . . ." can make a difference. Then follow up with factual statements. Drivers appreciate the change in conversational ambience when you begin using such phrases as: "My *objective* in doing this is . . ." "My *plan* for the next quarter . . ." "As I've *analyzed* the situation . . ." "A *logical conclusion* . . ." Why not use words and phrases that are music to a Driver's ears?
5. *Don't upset yourself over the Driver's impersonal and unfeeling manner.* If a Driver seems distant or disengaged, don't take it personally unless you have reason to believe you've done something to offend. People of this style tend to be more impersonal than below-the-line styles. Accept that this is the way these people are and that it's OK for them to be this way. You make things far worse if

you create judgmental labels about them in your mind or start telling yourself how unpleasant they are to work with.

Plan Your Work and Work Your Plan

The no-nonsense Driver wants everyone to be clear on goals and how they are going to be achieved. The more spontaneous Expressive is rarely as explicit about these things as the Driver expects. It's often a source of considerable tension.

1. *Convert your dreams into goals and objectives.* Push yourself to commit to a specific result.
2. *Be realistic.* Expressives are great optimists. In their enthusiasm, Expressives often set unattainable goals and objectives. However, Drivers want figures they can count on. So do set stretch goals— and make sure the goals are achievable.
3. *Plan your work.* Drivers are bare-bones planners, but they are planners nonetheless. Expressives have the least affinity for planning of all the styles. But you can do it. The Driver doesn't want you to waste time crafting ornate plans. Just come up with a simple, straightforward, results-oriented guide to action.
4. *Deliver the goods.* When Drivers specify objectives and draw up plans, their direction is set. They take great pride in delivering what they said they would—on standard, on schedule, and on budget. They expect others to do the same. It's not enough to plan your work; work your plan as well. You may be tired of that cliché, but when you heed it you'll have much better working relationships with Drivers.

Be Well Organized in Your Communication

When you communicate with Drivers, they expect you to be well organized, practical, factual, and brief. Expressives, however, are often poorly organized, somewhat impractical, less factual, and somewhat long-winded. That's a big communication chasm to bridge. When presenting ideas or recommendations to Drivers, you make your case better when you incorporate the following behaviors.

1. *Be prepared.* Drivers expect you to make good use of their time. Don't wing it; think things through in advance. Anticipate questions you may be asked. Even for one-on-one meetings, it's often appropriate to create an agenda. Most of the suggestions below are enhanced by using more than your customary preparation.
2. *Have a well-organized presentation.* Explain your thoughts system-

atically. It often helps to present your ideas as a series of points arranged in a logical order.

3. *When making recommendations, offer two options for the Driver.* Provide information that helps the Driver assess the probable outcome of each alternative.

4. *Focus on the results of the actions being discussed.* Very early in the discussion of alternative courses of action, describe possible outcomes of the approaches you describe. Then, factually demonstrate that the outcomes you project are both desirable and achievable.

5. *Be pragmatic.* Demonstrate to these practical people that your recommendations are very workable, no-frills ways of getting the results they want.

6. *Provide accurate factual evidence.* When talking with Drivers, it's rarely advisable to use someone's opinion or recommendation as evidence. Hard, accurate facts persuade these folks, so keep your presentation objective. Don't rely on sentiment or emotional appeals. As the detective on TV's *Dragnet* series used to say, "Just the facts . . . just the facts."

Avoid Power Struggles

The Driver is more assertive than most people. You are too. Because of that, the two of you have much in common. However, when two such assertive people work together, there's always the danger that sparks will fly. If that begins to happen, temporarily find ways of being less assertive. Listen more and listen better (pages 162–163). Decrease your vocal intensity, phrase your ideas more provisionally and be more negotiable (page 164).

In your initial efforts to flex to Drivers, you'll probably find it helpful to review the portrait of the Driver style found in Chapter Six, pages 43–46.

Flexing to Analyticals

As an Expressive, you differ from the Analytical on both dimensions of style. The Analytical is both less assertive and less responsive than you. So you may experience more style-based differences with Analyticals than with either Drivers or Amiables, each of whom has one of the basic dimensions of behavior in common with you. As a result there are more types of behavior you can modify when flexing to an Analytical than when flexing to any other style.

As you examine the following temporary adjustments of behavior that help you get in sync with Analyticals, select carefully the one to four types you think will help you work best with the particular person you're relating to. It's not easy to change habitual behavior, even for a short time, so *be sure to select only one to four types of behavior to work on.* Within each type or category of behavior, a number of specifics are mentioned. Do several, but not necessarily all, of the specifics within the behavioral categories you plan to emphasize. You'll probably think of additional ways to work better with the particular Analytical you'll be flexing to.

Slow Your Pace

For the Analytical, the fast pace of a typical Expressive is very uncomfortable. It throws Analyticals off their stride. If you want to work better with Analyticals, slow down and get more in sync with their natural rhythm.

1. *Talk slower.* When Expressives talk at their natural pace, Analyticals often have to strain to keep up. This is certainly not a user-friendly way of speaking with people. Why put yourself at that disadvantage when making a point?
2. *Don't create unnecessarily tight deadlines.* Remember, it can be very stressful for the Analytical to do things at your pace.
3. *When it comes to decision making, don't rush the Analytical unnecessarily.* There are times when these slow deciders need a nudge. But unless time is of the essence, let them make decisions their way: deliberately.

Listen More, Listen Better

Expressives tend to speak their minds; Analyticals are apt to keep their opinions to themselves. If the Expressive is also a poor listener, which is often the case, the Analytical is apt to clam up even more. It's hard to have a productive work relationship when one person is doing most of the talking. The Analytical's active participation begins to dry up, and the Expressives don't get the information they need. A growing rift appears in the relationship. Though the conversational lopsidedness is not all your fault, it's certainly in your best interest to improve the situation by listening more and better.

1. *Talk less.* When you're with an Analytical who tends to be on the quiet side, make a disciplined effort to talk less. Expressives who commit to having balanced conversations with Analyticals are usually helped by the method described in Chapter Eleven, "Antidote to Domineering: Listen Better and Speak Provisionally,"

pages 89–91. Although the section in Chapter Eleven was written for Drivers, the method is equally useful for Expressives.

2. *Provide more and longer pauses to make it easier for the Analytical to get into the conversation.* Analyticals need a longer pause than Expressives, so give them longer and more frequent pauses.

3. *Invite Analyticals to speak.* Request their input on the agenda; ask their opinion on the topics you cover. When explaining your thoughts, draw them into the conversation with checking questions: "How does this fit with your thinking?" "I'm interested in your point of view on what I've said." "How does this sound to you?"

4. *Reflect back to the speaker the gist of what you hear.* This is a way of acknowledging a person's viewpoint without either agreeing or disagreeing with it. Once you've reflected back what the person has said, pause to see if he wishes to add anything. Then it's your turn to give your response. Begin by stating points of agreement. Choose your words carefully if you disagree with parts of what the Analytical said. If people of this style think they'll get clobbered when they speak up, you'll hear even less from them in the future.

5. *Don't interrupt.* When you cut off another person in midsentence to add more comments of your own, it's not unreasonable for that person to assume you don't value his opinion. That can be a real barrier to constructive work relationships.

6. *Don't finish other people's sentences.* It can try the patience of a fast-paced Expressive to listen to the hesitant speech of a particularly slow-talking Analytical. But patience is a prime requisite for an Expressive who wants to flex effectively to an Analytical.

Don't Come on Too Strong

Analyticals, by definition, are less assertive than you. Their body language isn't as forceful. They don't speak as often and when they do they're not as emphatic. So when you use your normal Expressive behavior, the mismatch in assertiveness may lead the Analytical to think of you as pushy. A work relationship certainly isn't enhanced when one person feels she is being pushed around by another. Also, if your way of communicating makes you seem dogmatic, the Analytical may become even more silent than usual, thus depriving you of important information. Here are some things you can do to avoid coming on too strong to Analyticals.

1. *Decrease the intensity of your eye contact.* When speaking to an Analytical, look away a bit more than you normally would. And when you do make eye contact, soften your gaze.

2. *Limit your gestures.* Analyticals gesture less often and less energetically than any of the styles. They are often distracted and even disconcerted by an Expressive's frequent, large, and forceful gestures. So when you are working with Analyticals, tone down your body English considerably.

3. *Decrease your vocal intensity.* Soft-spoken Analyticals find it irritating when someone speaks to them in a loud voice during a normal conversation. You get through to this style much more effectively when you lower your voice.

4. *Lean back when you make a point.* Do as they do and lean back when you're talking. Fortunately, when you assume a more laid-back posture, you show less intensity in your eye contact, gestures, and voice.

5. *Phrase your ideas more provisionally.* Analyticals often choose language that's quite tentative. Expressives, however, may select words that suggest a more dogmatic stance than they mean to take. This kind of phrasing coupled with a fairly insistent body language may sound as if you are trying to rule out any discussion of the matter. These are some phrases that can help you come across in a less dogmatic manner: "Here's an idea off the top of my head." "I'd like to run this up the flagpole." "I like that idea. What if we also . . ." When you don't agree with something, you can take an approach like this: "I'd like to play devil's advocate for a few minutes."

6. *Be more negotiable.* When possible, avoid imposing your solution to a problem on your Analytical co-worker. Instead, use a win-win style of negotiation or cooperative problem solving to jointly create solutions to the problems you encounter.

Be More Task-Oriented

Analyticals are more task-oriented; Expressives are more people-oriented. Since tasks are performed by people, when used well either approach can be effective. In working with an Analytical, you may want to give increased attention to the task side of things.

1. *Be on time.* Analyticals are much more time-conscious than the average Expressive. So when working with Analyticals, watch your clock (and your calendar!) and be on time.

2. *Be a bit more formal.* In their clothing and grooming, Analyticals tend to be the most conservative of styles. You may want to have a somewhat conservative appearance when working with them. Also, don't be too flip or offbeat in your interactions with Analyticals. They usually expect a more buttoned-down type of work

relationship. Finally, your Analytical colleagues are more comfortable with you when you maintain a somewhat reserved demeanor with them.

3. *Get right to business.* Don't give the impression that you're there to chat. But don't lose your human touch, either. Limit the small talk. It's usually appropriate to spend a little time on openers, but keep it brief and don't make it too personal. Then get right into what you're there to talk about.

Deemphasize Feelings

Analyticals are less emotionally aware and less disclosing of their feelings than most people. You can get more in sync with Analyticals by being *less* emotionally disclosing. Be more reserved, without becoming cold or aloof.

1. *Limit your facial expressiveness.* Have your facial expression be a closer match to your co-worker's seriousness.
2. *Avoid touch.* Above-the-line people, like Analyticals, typically feel uneasy when someone touches them. Honor their preferences and avoid touch.
3. *Talk about what you think rather than about what you feel.* Think longer and harder about issues you're discussing with an Analytical. The words you use are important, too. Saying "I *think* . . ." instead of "I *feel* . . ." can make a difference. Then follow up with factual statements. Analyticals appreciate the change in conversational ambience when you begin using phrases such as: "I've *analyzed* the situation . . ." "My *objective* in doing this is . . ." "My *plan* for the next quarter . . ." "A *logical conclusion* . . ." Why not use words and phrases that are music to an Analytical's ears?
4. *Don't upset yourself over the Analytical's impersonal and unfeeling manner.* If the Analytical you are with seems distant or disengaged, don't take it personally unless you have reason to believe you've done something to offend. People of this style tend to be more impersonal than below-the-line styles. Accept that this is the way these people are and that it's OK for them to be this way. You make things far worse if you create judgmental labels about them in your mind, or start telling yourself how bad they are or how unpleasant they are to work with.

Be Systematic

Analyticals like to be systematic about most things they're associated with. Expressives prefer a much less regimented approach. This is often a point of tension between people of these styles. When you work with Analyticals, they find the relationship much more congenial when you are more systematic than usual.

1. *Set high standards.* Analyticals are the most quality-conscious of the styles. They like to base their systems on exceptionally high standards. Analyticals are partial to highly demanding standards like zero defects. So stretch as much as you can in setting standards for your work. Just be sure to deliver what you say you will. Analyticals get turned off sooner than most when someone makes a promise and doesn't deliver.
2. *Plan your work.* Analyticals are avid planners and like to work with people who develop detailed, step-by-step written plans.
3. *Work your plan.* Many Analyticals think of a plan as a rational road to accomplishment—and something that should be strictly adhered to. Consider being more organized than usual, without necessarily being as rigorous as the Analytical might wish.
4. *Develop superior procedures.* One way Analyticals try to achieve outstanding quality is through superior procedures and processes. When it comes to ongoing activities, they like co-workers to discover the best way of doing a task and then create a step-by-step procedure which, when followed, consistently yields excellent results. Chances are, you can find some areas in which new procedures are needed. When you develop them, you probably enhance productivity and build stronger ties to the Analyticals with whom you work.
5. *Continuously improve procedures.* Even more than most people, Analyticals are concerned with continuous improvement. Support their quest for quality by improving some of the most important procedures in your area.
6. *Be more rigorous in following established procedures.* Make the effort to think of procedures that would produce better results if you followed them more consistently. Doing so undoubtedly strengthens your relationship with the Analyticals in your work group.

Be Well Organized, Detailed, and Factual

Analyticals, the most perfectionistic of the styles, are particular about the way things are presented to them. They expect you to be well organized, detailed, and factual in your communication. Expressives, however, are often poorly organized, speak in generalities, and are less factual. That's a big communication chasm to bridge. In presenting ideas or making recommendations to Analyticals, you make your case better when you incorporate the following behaviors.

1. *Be prepared.* Analyticals expect you to make good use of their time. Don't wing it; think things through in advance. Dig up all the data you need. Anticipate questions you may be asked. Even for one-on-one meetings, it's often appropriate to create an agenda. Consider getting the agenda to the Analytical in advance; she may want to think about the topics beforehand. Most of the suggestions below are enhanced by using more than your customary preparation.

2. *Have a well-organized presentation.* Explain your thoughts systematically. It often helps to present your ideas as a series of points arranged in logical order; that's what Analyticals often do. You frequently hear them say, "In the first place . . . in the second place . . ." and so forth. When communicating with an Analytical, do likewise.

3. *Go into considerable detail.* When making a presentation to people of this style, don't just hit the high points. Analyticals want to delve into the particulars; they thrive on specifics. They want to make sure all the ground has been covered before they make a decision. You gain credibility with people of this style when they see that you've chased down every detail.

4. *Give a sound rationale for narrowing the options.* Analyticals want to consider all the alternatives. While this tendency often helps them make good decisions, it also increases their tendency to be inordinately indecisive. You can help them weed out some of the weaker alternatives by giving them logical and factual reasons for doing so.

5. *Mention the problems and disadvantages of the proposal you put forth.* In addition to mentioning the pluses of the proposition you recommend, tell them about the downside, too. The Analytical respects you for doing so. Then, build your credibility further by recommending ways of dealing with the problems and disadvantages.

6. *Show why the approach you advocate is best.* For Analyticals, "best" is a combination of quality, economy, and low risk. You have to figure out the relative weight of each of these criteria for a particular Analytical in a particular set of circumstances. "Best" for this style includes *long-term benefits* as well as immediate advantages. Discuss the future in terms of probabilities: "Here's a projection of what's likely to happen. . . ." The Analytical is conservative when it comes to risk, so if possible show why your approach is a fairly safe bet.

7. *Provide accurate factual evidence.* When talking with Analyticals, it's rarely advisable to use someone's opinion or recommendation as evidence. Hard facts persuade these folks. Since they like

an objective presentation, avoid emotional appeals. People of this style are both precise and skeptical; they abhor a superficial gathering of information or careless reporting of it. Where others might settle for approximations, Analyticals want meticulously correct information. So be painstakingly accurate in what you report to people of this style.

8. *Stick to business.* Don't digress. As you discuss the business at hand and are reminded of things that are tangential to the discussion, don't pursue these side issues.

9. *Provide written support materials, and/or follow up in writing.* Analyticals tend to prefer the written word to the spoken. Even so, it's best to make an oral presentation. That way you can note the Analytical's reactions and answer his questions. At the same time, cater to the Analytical's preference for written communication by preparing well-thought-out support materials and/or a follow-up report. If a decision was reached, you may want to include a step-by-step timetable for implementation.

10. *Be prepared to listen to far more detail than you want to know.* When Analyticals talk, they often present far more information than most people think is necessary. They explain their ideas or discuss progress on projects in what may feel like overwhelming detail. This much minutiae may be boring, especially for an Expressive, but be patient and try to stay tuned in. Analyticals appreciate your attentiveness. And there's probably information you need to know buried somewhere in all that detail.

In your initial efforts to flex to Analyticals, you'll probably find it helpful to review the portrait of the Analytical style found in Chapter Six, pages 30–33.

Relating to Other Expressives

When people of the same style work together, they may be too similar! They lack important differences that occur when people of two or more styles collaborate. Some of these style-based differences can be useful at times in developing productive work relationships. Thus when relating to another Expressive, you may sometimes find it advantageous to temporarily use behaviors that are more characteristic of one of the other styles. For example, Expressives are often entertaining. When a couple of Expressives are working together, they may be more productive if one becomes more serious. Also, Expressives typically focus on the big picture. When two Expressives are collaborating, it's often helpful if one calls their attention to details. One of the two Expressives could help them both focus more on a systematic approach. Similarly, Expressives are so out-front and talkative that when they are engaged in a project they may become less productive over time, because neither of them puts in the effort required to listen and allow the other to shine, too. Or they may come up with a visionary recommendation that ultimately fails because they paid scant attention to the needs in the styles of the people who would have to implement the plan.

Therefore, in relating to another Expressive, make sure you don't overuse style-based tendencies or use them when it's inappropriate to do so. Also, look for times to add some of the strengths more characteristic of the other styles by temporarily modifying some of your behavior.

When two highly assertive Expressives work together, there's always a danger that they'll end up in a power struggle. This is the biggest threat to Expressive-Expressive relationships. If you find that you and another Expressive are beginning to butt heads together, temporarily find ways of being less assertive. Listen more and listen better (pages 162–163). Decrease your vocal intensity, phrase your ideas more provisionally, and be more negotiable (pages 163–164).

Appendix IV

For *Analyticals* Only: How to Flex to Each Style

The purpose of Appendix IV is to coach Analyticals on specific things they can do to create more productive relationships with people of each style.

Most of the recommendations are temporary behavioral changes that you can make for a few minutes, before resuming your more comfortable style-based ways. However, we also mention a few options, such as speaking up more often, that could become more of an ongoing part of your behavioral repertoire.

Since this appendix is a planning aid, don't try to read it straight through. Instead, find the section that applies to the style you want to flex to:

- Drivers, page 170
- Amiables, page 174
- Expressives, page 178
- Other Analyticals, page 186

Read that section and figure out what you can do to help people of that style work more effectively with you. Later, when you want to improve your relationship with someone of a different style, read the section dealing with that style. By working your way through the Appendix on an as-needed basis, you'll soon read all sections and strengthen important relationships in the process.

Flexing to Drivers

As an Analytical you have much in common with Drivers. You are similar on one of the two basic dimensions of style: Both of you are less responsive than most people. Consequently, Drivers tend to appreciate your focus on task and your objective approach to things.

In flexing to a Driver, your major challenge is to get in sync with some of her more assertive behavior. You should be able to create a more effective working relationship with a Driver by *temporarily* using some of the following six types of behavior, within each of which a number of specifics are mentioned. Do several, but not necessarily all, of the specifics within the types of behavior you plan to emphasize. You'll probably think of additional ways to work better with the specific Driver you have in mind.

Pick up the Pace

Drivers tend to do everything at a fast pace. Analyticals move and speak slowly. You'll usually relate better to Drivers when you increase your pace considerably.

1. *Move more quickly than usual.* Walk at a faster pace. Do whatever you are doing as quickly as possible—on the double when you flex to a Driver.
2. *Speak more rapidly* than is normal for you. Also, pause less often.
3. *Use time efficiently.* When meeting with a Driver, don't exceed the allotted time. Do your business at a fast clip. Then leave quickly yet graciously.
4. *Address problems quickly.* When problems arise, face them and dispose of them as soon as possible. From the Driver's point of view, there's no time like the present to resolve a troubled situation.
5. *Be prepared to decide quickly.* Knowing that the Driver makes decisions quickly, anticipate decisions he wants from you (or will want to make with you) and do whatever preparation you can to speed your decision making.
6. *Implement decisions as soon as possible.* Once a decision is made, try to put it into operation immediately. Drivers are do-it-now people. When you are action-oriented, they're less stressed.
7. *Complete projects on schedule.* More than any other style, Drivers value on-time completion. So don't miss deadlines. When you commit to a schedule, especially with a Driver, keep your commitment.
8. *Respond promptly to messages and requests.*
9. *When writing, keep it short.* Consider "bulleting" key points. Put supporting information in appendixes.

Demonstrate Higher Energy

Drivers are typically high-energy people. Analyticals, by contrast, display less energy than most people. When relating to Drivers, there are times when you'll need to put more energy into what you say and do.

1. *Lean into the conversation.* Keep your back straight and lean into the conversation. Keep your feet flat on the floor. Keep your head erect, not propped on your hands.
2. *Use gestures to show your involvement in the conversation.* Analyticals tend to gesture less than any of the other styles. Use more emphatic body English.
3. *Increase the frequency and intensity of your eye contact.*
4. *Increase your vocal intensity.* Speak a bit louder than you normally would. Show conviction through your voice. Let your vocal intensity communicate that you are taking the matter seriously.
5. *Move and speak more quickly.* The behaviors suggested under the heading "Pick Up the Pace" all help you interact more energetically.

Don't Get Bogged Down in Details or Theory

As an Analytical, you probably want a more detailed understanding of most things than people of the other styles do. Also, Analyticals have more of a theoretical bent than most people. When relating to a Driver, keep to a minimum any discussion of details or theory.

1. *Concentrate on high-priority issues.* Drivers seldom want to be briefed on as many topics as an Analytical may want to discuss.
2. *Present the main points and skip all but the most essential details.* The Driver will ask for more information if wanted. Assume that the Driver is interested in only a fraction of the information you might find interesting or important.
3. *Don't get side-tracked in theory or in recounting the history of the problem or the solution.* Drivers are not particularly interested in the theoretical and historical aspects of an issue. If it is truly necessary to touch on the history of a situation or the theory behind your approach, cover these matters quickly while showing their relevance to achieving the desired result. Then move quickly to more down-to-earth subject matter.

Say What You Think

Drivers tend to speak up and express themselves candidly and directly. Analyticals are apt to keep their thoughts to themselves and speak somewhat tentatively and indirectly. Here's how you can bridge that behavioral gap.

1. *Speak up more often.* Initiate conversations more frequently. In conversations and meetings, express yourself frequently enough so

that there's a more balanced give-and-take. Drivers usually want to know where people stand. They would rather not have to try to interpret the meaning of your silence or have to pry thoughts out of you.

2. *Tell more; ask less.* Say, "Here's what I think . . ." rather than "Do you think it would make sense to . . . ?" Say "Please do this" instead of "Could you do this?"

3. *Make statements that are definite rather than tentative.* Avoid words like *try, perhaps, maybe, possibly,* etc. Be specific. Don't say you'll complete a project "as soon as possible"; say it will be done "by 12:00 noon next Tuesday."

4. *Eliminate gestures that suggest you lack confidence in the point you are making.* Don't shrug your shoulders, hold your palms up, or use facial expressions that undercut what you are saying, imply helplessness, or suggest the avoidance of responsibility.

5. *Voice your disagreements.* Drivers are more accustomed to conflict than Analyticals are. Face conflict more openly; state your opinion frankly but tactfully. At the same time, try to avoid situations where you and the Driver are battling from entrenched positions.

6. *Don't gloss over problems.* Beat bad news to the punch. Then give regular, brief, frank reports on your progress regarding the problem situation.

Speak in Practical, Results-Oriented Terms

There are important differences in what would be persuasive to a Driver and what would influence an Analytical. To get your point across to a Driver, emphasize what's convincing to her.

1. *Focus on the results of the action being discussed.* Very early in the discussion of a course of action, describe the outcomes that could be achieved by the approach you advocate. Then, factually demonstrate that the outcome you project is both desirable and achievable.

2. *Emphasize that it's a pragmatic approach.* Analyticals, in their quest for perfection, often seek the best solution even though something less costly or less time-consuming might do just fine. Drivers, in searching for a solution, often opt for something that is less than the best as long as it will do the job. Take a hard-headed approach when discussing solutions with a Driver.

Facilitate Self-Determination

Drivers are very self-directed. They want to do things their way. Although Analyticals are less assertive than half the population, they can be very precise about what they want done and the way they want it done. When Analyticals get highly specific about how things are to be done, Drivers often bridle at what seems to them like excessive control. Here are some ways Analyticals can constructively facilitate a Driver's sense of self-direction.

1. *Give the Driver as much freedom as possible in setting her own objectives.*
2. *As far as practicable, let the Driver determine how to do projects and achieve objectives.*
3. *When making recommendations, offer a couple of options for the Driver.* While an Analytical might want to consider additional alternatives, two options are usually enough to satisfy the Driver's desire to make a choice.
4. *When presenting options, provide a succinct factual summary* that helps the Driver assess the probable outcome of each alternative.
5. *Don't be a stickler for rules.* Drivers are prone to stretch or break rules in order to achieve results. When appropriate, be open to changing or bending the rules.

In your initial efforts to flex to Drivers, you'll probably find it helpful to review the portrait of the Driver style found in Chapter Six, pages 43–46.

Flexing to Amiables

As an Analytical, you have much in common with Amiables. You are similar on one of the two basic dimensions of style. Both of you are less assertive than most people. Amiables appreciate the similarity of your pacing and that you aren't as pushy as many more assertive people.

In flexing to an Amiable, your prime challenge is to get in sync with some of his more responsive behavior. You create a more effective working relationship with an Amiable by *temporarily* using some of the following types of behavior, within each of which a number of specifics are mentioned. Do several, but not necessarily all, of the specifics within the behavioral category you plan to emphasize. You'll probably think of additional ways to work better with the particular Amiable you have in mind.

Make Genuine Personal Contact

The Amiable wants to be treated as a human being and not as a function or a role only. The Analytical, who is more task-oriented than most people, may need to remember to show a sincere interest in the Amiable as a person.

1. *Don't seem aloof.* Without overdoing it, demonstrate more warmth in your words, your tone of voice, and your facial expression.
2. *When the situation permits, be more casual and informal* than usual. To Amiables, your tendency to be more formal than most other people may make you seem stiff and impersonal. Let your hair down a bit when with people of this style.
3. *At the outset, touch base personally.* When beginning a conversation, take a few minutes to build rapport. Show that you are interested in the Amiable as a person. Give Amiables an opening to talk about themselves.
4. *Disclose something about yourself.* The Amiable likes to invite you to talk about yourself. Don't brush it off with, "Oh, things are fine." Briefly, let her know something personal about yourself.
5. *Make the most of opportunities for conversations that are not task-related.* For example, when waiting for a meeting to begin, don't read a report; use that time to chat with Amiables and others who like more personal contact. When a meeting concludes, you can also create opportunities for social interchange. Find other occasions to be in touch with Amiables as people. The goal is to be appropriately though not excessively sociable.

Focus More on Feelings

Amiables are expressive of their emotions and sensitive to the feelings of others. You can get more in sync with Amiables by focusing more on feelings—both theirs and your own.

1. *Look at the person you are conversing with* so you can take in body-language cues. This is important because feelings are best discerned from nonverbals. This may take some effort on your part because, more than any other style, As an Analytical you tend to have less eye contact with the person you are talking to.
2. *Concentrate on the meaning of the person's body language.* Analyticals are apt to give excessive attention to the words that are spoken and overlook important nonverbal cues. Pay attention to the Amiable's nonverbal signals, and keep asking yourself, "What does this suggest about what this person may be feeling right now?"
3. *Note how the other person reacts.* Amiables dislike conflict and may not verbalize their disagreement or dissatisfaction. Changes in their body language can tip you off as to how they may be reacting to what is being said. Once you surmise that the other person has negative feelings about a proposal, you can invite his reaction: "Some people are leery of this part of the plan. I'm interested in your thoughts about it."

4. *Demonstrate more feelings yourself.* If you are pleased about something, say so. If you are disappointed, let that be known. Let your body language express your feelings more; put a bit more inflection into your voice. Smile more to demonstrate warmth toward the person you are with.

Be Supportive

Amiables are supportive of others, and they expect others to be supportive in turn. They feel that's the least that one human being should be able to expect from another.

1. *Listen empathically so the Amiable feels heard and understood.* To truly listen to another is one of the most supportive things we can do for a person.
2. *Express sincere appreciation for the Amiable's contributions.* Even more than most people, Amiables thrive on appreciation. Don't let your Analytical tendencies toward being perfectionistic and overly critical prevent you from seeing and acknowledging the good things the Amiable does. Also, decrease the number of critical and judgmental statements you make. When you do criticize, make sure it's constructive.
3. *Lend a helping hand.* Amiables are the most helpful of the People-Styles. They're apt to drop what they're doing to aid someone who's in a pinch. They appreciate it when you spot an opportunity to give them a hand when they're under pressure.

Provide Structure

Amiables tend to be most comfortable and work best in stable, clearly structured situations. Do what you can to contribute to that stability and structure.

1. When it's within your area of responsibility, *make sure the Amiable's job is well-defined and goals are clearly established.* Amiables work best when their roles are clarified and their goals are set.
2. *Help the Amiable plan difficult projects and design complex work processes.* Planning is not the Amiable's forte. When you help an Amiable develop a sound plan or design an effective work process, she usually takes it from there.
3. *Reduce uncertainty.* Amiables aren't likely to function well in highly ambiguous situations. Try not to put the Amiable in an unstable, rapidly fluctuating situation.
4. *Demonstrate loyalty.* In most cases Amiables feel a greater-than-

average loyalty to the people they work with and the organizations they work in. Consequently, they expect you to demonstrate your loyalty to them, their co-workers, and the organization. Amiables are turned off when they hear you take potshots at employees or the organization. Instead of voicing criticisms, make constructive suggestions for improvement and make them directly to the people involved.

Demonstrate Interest in the Human Side

Amiables tend to take a people-oriented approach whereas Analyticals are prone to be task-oriented. When working with an Amiable, give increased attention to the human side of things.

1. *Invite Amiables' input on matters that affect them.* Although they aren't as demanding as most people, they like to be consulted on matters pertaining to them.
2. *Discuss the effects of decisions on people and their morale.* Be alert to and speak about the effect on people of new policies, procedures, processes, and projects. For example, when discussing a new practice, in addition to pointing out its cost-cutting advantages, be sure to add: "Most people will like the way it cuts down on the excessive overtime they've been complaining about."
3. When appropriate, *provide an opportunity for the Amiable to talk with others* before committing to a decision.

Don't Overdo Facts and Logic

Analyticals find facts and logic highly convincing. Amiables don't find facts and logic as persuasive as you do. Oftentimes what seems like an appropriate amount of facts and logic to an Analytical is overkill to an Amiable.

1. *Edit out of your conversation any facts that aren't absolutely necessary to making your point.* You'll be surprised at how few are really needed.
2. *Don't overdo the appeal to logic.* It's not that Amiables are averse to logic, but they don't like it when someone piles reason upon reason to make his case. When Amiables feel that logic is being overused, they're likely to be bored or annoyed rather than persuaded.
3. *Don't be coercive in your use of facts and logic.* If you try to build an airtight case showing that the alternative you favor is the only way to go, the Amiable thinks your amassing of facts is not so much convincing as overly controlling.
4. *Show that other people support the idea you are advancing.* This people-oriented style is often influenced more by the experiences and opin-

ions of others than by cold facts. Provide evidence from experts. Mention testimonies of others who have successfully used a similar approach. The opinions of trusted colleagues is especially convincing.

5. *Note factors that minimize the risk* of the course of action you are proposing. To the degree possible, provide assurance that there will be no glitches. If there are guarantees, highlight them.

In your initial efforts to flex to Amiables, you'll probably find it helpful to review the portrait of the Amiable style found in Chapter Six, pages 33–38.

Flexing to Expressives

As an Analytical, you differ from the Expressive on both dimensions of style. The Expressive is both more assertive and more responsive than you. So you may experience more style-based differences with an Expressive than with either a Driver or an Amiable, each of whom has one of the basic dimensions of behavior in common with you. As a result there are more types of behavior that you can modify when flexing to an Expressive than when flexing to any other style.

As you read the types of temporary adjustment of behavior that help you get in sync with Expressives, select carefully the one to four types you think will help you work best with the particular person you're relating to. It's not easy to change habitual behavior, even for a short time, so *be sure to select only one to four types of behavior to work on.* Within each type or category of behavior, a number of specifics are mentioned. Do several, but not necessarily all, of the specifics within the behavioral categories you plan to emphasize. You'll probably think of additional ways to work better with the particular Expressive you'll be flexing to.

Make Personal Contact

Expressives like to have personal contact with those they work with. It's important to them that they get to know you and that you get to know them personally. Analyticals, who tend to focus more on the task aspects of things, need to remind themselves to take the time and make the effort to establish personal contact with Expressives they work with.

1. *Don't seem aloof.* Without overdoing it, demonstrate more warmth in your words, your tone of voice, and your facial expression.
2. *Be more casual and informal* than usual. Expressives are inclined to informality. To them, the tendency of Analyticals to be more formal than most people may make them seem stiff and impersonal. Let your hair down a bit in this conversation.

3. *At the outset, touch base personally.* Take a few minutes to build rapport at the beginning of a conversation. Show Expressives that you are interested in them as people; give them an opening to talk about themselves. Perhaps you can inquire about their personal interests or their opinions on a topic that's being widely discussed.
4. *Disclose something about yourself.* Expressives are the most talkative of the styles, so you may have to look for an opening to get in a word about yourself. You don't have to go on at length, but do let them get to know you better.
5. *Talk about what's going on with other people, too.* The gregarious Expressive is interested in knowing the latest about people she knows.
6. *Look for opportunities for conversations that are not task-related.* When a meeting ends, there may be a few minutes for the two of you to catch up on one another's life. The goal is to be appropriately though not excessively sociable.

Pick Up the Pace

Expressives talk fast, move quickly, and decide quickly. When it comes to implementation, they want it done yesterday. Expressives find it easier to work with you when you pick up the pace somewhat.

1. *Move more quickly than usual.* Walk at a faster pace. Do things on the double when you flex to an Expressive.
2. *Speak more rapidly than is normal for you.* Also, pause less often. Expressives are fast-paced talkers and are quickly bored when pace slackens.
3. *Don't over explain.* Present the main points and skip the details. The Expressive will ask for more information if it's wanted.
4. *Address problems quickly.* When problems arise, face them and dispose of them as soon as possible.
5. *Be ready to decide quickly.* Knowing that the Expressive makes decisions quickly, anticipate decisions he expects you to make (or will want to make with you) and do whatever preparation you can to speed your decision making.
6. *Implement as soon as possible.* Once a decision is made, put it into operation immediately.

Demonstrate Higher Energy

Expressives are usually brimming with energy; Analyticals show less energy than most people. When relating to Expressives, you may find it helpful at times to put more energy into what you say and do.

1. *Lean into the conversation.* When you do, you look much more alert and energetic than you do in the characteristic leaning-back mode of most Analyticals.
2. *Use more and bigger gestures.* Show your involvement in the conversation by using more body English. Gesture more frequently than is customary for you.
3. *Increase the frequency and intensity of your eye contact.* Expressives look you right in the eye when they talk to you. They expect you to do the same with them.
4. *Increase your vocal intensity.* Speak a bit louder than normal. Try putting more inflection in your voice; above all, don't speak in a monotone.
5. *Change your posture now and then.* Expressives always seem to be moving. Even when sitting, they don't sit still. They shift around in their chairs, tap a pencil, or fidget with a paper clip. So don't sit there like a bump on a log. Obviously, you want to avoid engaging in some of the Expressive's more distracting behavior, but you can change your posture now and then and gesture more.

Focus More on Feelings

Expressives are very in touch with and disclosing of their feelings. Whatever those feelings are, they influence and sometimes even dominate the Expressive's decisions, actions, and responses to others. Analyticals are seen as the least emotive of the styles, so relating well to Expressives' feelings is a key to working effectively with them.

1. *Be aware of what the Expressive is feeling.* It's not that an Expressive's emotional cues are apt to be subtle; they probably come across loud and clear. But everyone has selective perception, and the Analytical is likely to become engrossed in the *content* of the conversation and miss the emotional component even when it's quite obvious. Since the Expressive's emotions have a major impact on their decisions, actions, and reactions, it's crucial to stay in touch with what they're feeling.
2. *Acknowledge the Expressive's feelings.* When Expressives are "up" about something they're working on, acknowledge the feelings: "You're excited about the way project X is going." When they're down, reflect those feelings, too: "You're frustrated that just when you got Sandy trained, she was transferred to another department, and you'll have to start breaking in a new rep."
3. *Don't overreact to the Expressive's highs and lows.* Expressives have greater mood swings than any of the styles. When they're high, they are energetic and excited about what they're doing. When

they're low, they feel discouraged and unappreciated. As an Analytical, you are probably very even-keeled in emotional terms. Don't read too much into the Expressive's extremes of feeling unless they persist over time. An Expressive's feeling states are more fleeting than most people's; she will probably be in a very different mood shortly.

4. *Show more feelings yourself.* If you are delighted about something, say so; if you are disappointed, let that be known. When you're annoyed, you can say something like, "I'm irritated that you missed this deadline." Let your body language convey more of your feelings, too. When expressing feelings, put more inflection in your voice and gesture a bit more.

5. *Demonstrate more enthusiasm.* Although Expressives get dispirited at times, they are the most enthusiastic of the styles. Analyticals are so matter-of-fact that when they feel enthusiastic, it rarely shows. When working with an Expressive, it's important to let him see some of your enthusiasm. For example, when trying to sell an idea to an Expressive, your enthusiasm may be more persuasive than a logical presentation of the facts of the case. If you don't show excitement about the idea, the Expressive is apt to think you lack confidence in it. Also, when it's genuine, share your enthusiasm for the Expressive's projects and victories.

6. *Don't read too much into an Expressive's volatile verbal attacks.* Remember, under normal circumstances people of this style are very emotive and more given to exaggeration than any of the styles; when angry, both of these tendencies become more pronounced. What the Expressive says in anger often is an exaggeration. Try not to take the angry comments literally. The Expressive has more temper to control than most people, so don't assume the derogatory things said in a fit of anger accurately communicate her thinking. However, if the verbal abuse becomes excessive, find a way to put an end to it.

Cooperate With the Expressive's Conversational Spontaneity

It's important to realize that when Expressives talk, they're often "thinking out loud." When discussing their own conversational style, Expressives commonly say, "I speak to find out what I'm thinking." The Analytical, on the other hand, tends to think things through before speaking. If these differences in conversational style are not recognized and adapted to, communication snafus are probable.

1. *Allow enough time for the conversation.* Though Expressives' speech is fast-paced, their tendency to tell stories and skip from one topic

to another can be quite time consuming, so don't impose tight
time constraints on your meeting with an Expressive.

2. *Keep a balance between flowing with an Expressive's digressions and getting back on track.* With Expressives you can expect to have some long, wandering conversations. If you try to keep these highly assertive people from getting sidetracked onto other subjects, you're apt to end in an unproductive power struggle. However, after they've digressed for a while, you sometimes need to tactfully get the conversation refocused.

3. *Spend time in mutual exploration.* Once the Expressive gets enthusiastic about a solution, he may not want to explore other options. Similarly, you are apt to arrive at what you consider the best solution. But when the two of you argue from fixed positions, the result can be an unproductive "dialogue of the deaf." To avoid this, be sure to listen well and set up the conversation in such a way that there's a mutual discussion of the problem and possible solutions.

4. *Be patient with overstatements.* With their bias toward the dramatic, Expressives are likely to exaggerate to make a point. Unless a more accurate understanding of a particular matter is essential to the discussion, don't press for accuracy. Concentrate instead on the idea the Expressive is trying to get across, and let the conversation move on.

5. *Be tactful in responding to contradictions in what the Expressive says.* Since Expressives are thinking things through while they talk, they sometimes make contradictory statements in the same conversation without realizing it. If the conflicting thoughts are not germane to what's being discussed, just overlook the discrepancy. If it's central to what is being talked about, find a diplomatic way to get at the actual meaning of the Expressive's statements.

Be Open to the Expressive's Fun-Loving Side

Expressives are the most playful and fun-loving of the styles. They like to mix pleasure with business. The Analytical, on the other hand, is the most serious of the four styles. If you lighten up a little when working with an Expressive, you may be able to get more done than if you take a nose-to-the-grindstone approach.

1. *Don't get impatient if the Expressive indulges in a few jokes.* When you are ready to get down to business, an Expressive is apt to regale you with jokes. Instead of getting upset at what might seem like a waste of time, relax and enjoy the humor. There's no need for you

to get into the act with jokes of your own, though. Analytical humor doesn't necessarily entertain an Expressive.

2. *Be relaxed about a certain amount of fooling around.* Even in the midst of serious business, an Expressive may engage in horseplay. Go with the flow for a while. It may be the release the Expressive needs before focusing again on the business at hand.

3. *Try to create a more pleasant atmosphere for your conversation.* Sitting behind a table in a sterile conference room or talking across a desk in someone's office is not the Expressive's cup of tea. So, if the weather and location permit, talk while taking a noontime stroll, or over breakfast or lunch at a favorite bistro. . . . Put your mind to it, and you'll find more options than you expect.

Give the Expressive Recognition

Expressives, even more than most people, enjoy recognition.

1. *Show appreciation for the Expressive's contribution.* Expressives thrive on sincere compliments. For the Expressive, it's even better if the appreciation is expressed publicly.

2. *Let the Expressive be in the spotlight.* By and large, people of this style find it easy to be the center of attention. Try to find ways for them to get the recognition they enjoy while making sure everyone on a project gets the credit they deserve.

Say What You Think

Expressives usually say what they are feeling and thinking. Their speech is direct; their statements are definite and they are emphatic much of the time. Analyticals are apt to keep their thoughts to themselves and speak somewhat tentatively and indirectly. Here's how you can bridge that behavioral gap.

1. *Speak up more often.* Expressives, being the most verbal of the styles, enjoy having more than 50 percent of the air time. On the other hand, they usually want to know where people stand and would rather not have to interpret the meaning of your silence or have to pry thoughts out of you. So initiate conversations more frequently. In conversations and meetings, express yourself more so that there's a somewhat balanced give-and-take.

2. *Tell more; ask less.* Say "Here's what I think . . ." rather than "Do you think it would make sense to . . . ?" Say "Please do this" instead of "Could you do this?"

3. *Make statements that are definite rather than tentative.* Avoid words

like *try, perhaps, maybe, possibly,* etc. Be specific. Don't say you'll complete a project "as soon as possible"; say it will be done "by 12:00 noon next Tuesday."

4. *Eliminate gestures that suggest you lack confidence in what you are saying.* Don't shrug your shoulders, hold your palms up, or use facial expressions that undercut what you are saying, imply helplessness, or suggest the avoidance of responsibility.

5. *Voice your disagreements.* Expressives are more accustomed to conflict than Analyticals are. Face conflict more openly. State your opinion frankly. It's generally OK to let some of your temper show when you are in a conflict with Expressives. However, the highly competitive Expressive loves to win arguments. So don't let your disagreement degenerate into an argument. One option you have is to explore alternative solutions jointly, searching for one that meets both people's needs.

6. *Don't gloss over problems.* Beat bad news to the punch. Then give regular, frank reports on your progress regarding the problem situation.

Communicate on the Expressive's Wavelength

When speaking with an Expressive, realize that information you find convincing may carry little weight with the Expressive. Here are some ways to communicate on the Expressive's wavelength.

1. *Communicate face-to-face.* If you want your ideas to get a fair hearing with an Expressive, talk things over face-to-face. If that's not possible, try using the telephone. When you reach a definite conclusion in your face-to-face meeting or phone call, paraphrase it. Then, on important matters, follow up immediately with a *brief* written summary of what was decided.

2. *Try to support the Expressive's vision.* People of this style tend to be dreamers—in both the best and the worst senses of the word. They often have a vision of a better future for their department or organization. But their vision may be unrealistic or poorly aligned with the direction of the corporation. When you can, help Expressives inject realism into their proposed ventures. And on those occasions when you can't conscientiously support their visionary proposals, be respectful as well as clear in expressing your opposition.

3. *Focus on the big picture.* Analyticals are inclined to dig into the nitty-gritty of an issue; Expressives are mainly interested in the big picture. They have limited concern about specifics and they don't thrive on complexity. They go for the KIS formula: Keep It

Simple. To the degree that the subject matter allows, when talking with an Expressive give an overview and skip the details. When Expressives want to know more, they'll ask.

4. *Don't overdo facts and logic.* What seems like a desirable amount of facts and logic to an Analytical seems like overkill to an Expressive. Edit out of your conversation any facts or logic that aren't absolutely essential to making your point; you'll be surprised at how little is really needed. Also, skip as much of the historical development and theoretical background as can be eliminated.

5. *Highlight recommendations of others*—especially recommendations of people the Expressive knows and respects. The testimony of people who have successfully used the same approach probably carries more weight than tables of statistics or other impersonal evidence.

6. *Demonstrate concern about the human side.* When possible, invite the Expressive's input before a decision is made. Discuss the effect on people of new policies, procedures, processes, and projects.

7. *Recommend a particular course of action.* Rather than present Expressives with options, it's often best to help them get enthused about what seems to be the best alternative.

8. *Provide incentives* when possible. Everybody likes an incentive, but few people are as motivated by them as Expressives.

Provide Considerable Freedom

Expressives are free spirits. When their improvisational spirit meets the Analytical's desire for precise systems and careful planning, there's a considerable gap to be bridged.

1. *Help Expressives put their personal stamp on what they do.* They want their work to be a form of self-expression. Regarding the things they are involved with, they want to be able to say, "I did it my way." However, Analyticals are often very precise about how they want things done. When possible, avoid pressuring the Expressive into doing things your way.

2. *Empower Expressives to do new things.* They hate doing the same old things in the same old ways. Look for ways to help them inject some novelty into their work. Also, try to find new approaches to the way the two of you work together.

3. *Don't be a stickler for rules.* More than most people, Expressives don't like rules. They hate red tape and are quick to stretch or break the rules, whether for their own convenience, to increase productivity, or to better serve a customer. So when you can, relax your own tendency to go by the book.

4. *Be willing to improvise when you can.* Although you probably want to plan your work and work your plan, for the Expressive, planning is a drag and following a plan feels like being put in a straitjacket. Be open to the possibility of winging it from time to time.

5. *Cater to their physical restlessness.* Expressives hate to sit still. So don't just sit and talk with an Expressive for long periods; create reasons to get up and move around a bit. Also, since Expressives don't like the confinement of a desk-type job, whenever it's in your power, help them find projects or roles that enable them to release some of their physical energy.

In your initial efforts to flex to Expressives, you'll probably find it helpful to review the portrait of the Expressive style found in Chapter Six, pages 38–43.

Relating to Other Analyticals

When people of the same style work together, they may be too similar! They lack important differences that occur when people of two or more styles collaborate. Some of these style-based differences can be useful at times in developing productive work relationships. Thus when relating to another Analytical, you may sometimes find it advantageous to temporarily use behaviors that are more characteristic of one of the other styles. For example, Analyticals are often indecisive. When two Analyticals are working together, they may be more productive if one becomes more decisive. Also, Analyticals tend to be exceptionally focused on details. When two Analyticals are collaborating, it's often helpful if one challenges the need for so much detail. One of the two Analyticals could help them both focus more on the big picture. Similarly, Analyticals are so task-oriented that when two of them are engaged in a project, they may become less productive over time because neither of them puts in the effort required to maintain a good working relationship. Or they may come up with a sound recommendation that ultimately fails because they paid scant attention to the human side of the change they proposed.

Therefore, in relating to another Analytical, make sure you don't overuse style-based tendencies or use them when it's inappropriate to do so. Also, look for times to add some of the strengths more characteristic of the other styles by temporarily modifying some of your behavior.

More than most people, Analyticals have a need to be *right.* Unless this tendency is tempered, it makes them less open to other people's ideas and less negotiable than most people. So even though Analyticals are less assertive than most people, when two of them work together, it's not unusual for them to get locked in a power struggle about the way to proceed. If you find that you and an Analytical co-worker are getting deadlocked about issues, listen more and listen better. Phrase your ideas more provisionally and be more negotiable. Some tips on how to do these things are found in Appendix II, pages 143–144 and 144–145. Although the tips in that appendix are written for Drivers, you'll be able to apply them to your situation.

Notes

Chapter One: No Wonder We Have People Problems

1. The examples in this book are drawn from the experiences of real people. Names and some details have been altered to preserve confidentiality.
2. Morgan McCall, Jr., and Michael Lombardo, "What Makes a Top Executive?" *Psychology Today*, February 1983, pp. 26–31.

Chapter Two: People Are More Predictable Than You Think

1. Hamilton Jordan, *Crisis: The Last Years of the Carter Presidency* (New York: G. P. Putnam's Sons, 1982), p. 369.
2. Marilyn Ferguson, *The Aquarian Conspiracy: Personal and Social Transformation in the 1980s* (Los Angeles: J. P. Tarcher, 1980) pp. 298–299. Italicized in the original.

Chapter Four: Two Keys to Understanding People

1. Warner Wolf, with William Taffee, *Gimmee a Break!* (New York: Avon Books, 1983), p. 127.
2. David Merrill and Roger Reid, *Personal Styles and Effective Performance* (Radnor, Pa.: Chilton, 1981), p. 219.
3. Paul Ekman, *Telling Tales* (New York: W. W. Norton, 1976), pp. 125–126.

Chapter Six: Four Paths to Success

1. Peter Drucker, *Management: Tasks, Responsibilities, Practices* (New York: Harper & Row, 1973), p. 616.

Chapter Seven: Styles Under Stress

1. Leo Buscaglia, *Loving, Living, and Learning* (New York: Holt, Rinehart & Winston, 1982), p. 97.

Chapter Eight: Finding Common Ground With People

1. Everett Shostrom, *Man, The Manipulator: The Inner Journey From Manipulation to Actualization* (Nashville, Tenn.: Abingdon Press, 1967), p. 15.
2. Maxie Dunnam, Gary Herbertson, and Everett Shostrom, *The Manipulator and the Church* (Nashville, Tenn.: Abingdon Press, 1967), p. 25. Italicized in the original.
3. Frederick Perls, *In and Out the Garbage Pail* (Moab, Utah: Real People Press, 1969).
4. Reuel Howe, *Man's Need and God's Action* (Greenwich, Conn.: Seabury, 1953), p. 24.
5. Lewis Thomas, *Late Night Thoughts on Listening to Mahler's Ninth Symphony* (New York: Viking, 1983), p. 128.
6. Boris Pasternak, *Doctor Zhivago* (New York: Pantheon, 1958).
7. Nathaniel Branden, *Honoring the Self* (Los Angeles: Jeremy P. Tarcher, 1983), p. 58.
8. Erich Fromm, *Psychoanalysis and Religion* (New Haven, Conn.: Yale University Press, 1950), p. 74.
9. John Love, *McDonald's: Behind the Arches* (New York: Bantam, 1986), p. 145.
10. Clifford Notorius and Howard Markham, *We Can Work It Out: Making Sense of Marital Conflict* (New York: G. P. Putnam & Sons, 1993), p. 29. Italicized in the original. Their research was on marriage and other intimate relationships.
11. David Merrill, Roger Reid, and their associates developed the concept of *versatility*, which was the starting point for our thinking about *interpersonal flexibility*. We are indebted to the pioneering work these industrial psychologists did in this area. Our own point of view has evolved over time and now is considerably different from that of Merrill and Reid. For example, the term *style flex* is not used in their published work to date, and personal conversations with them suggest that this is not included in their thinking about versatility. Nor do they isolate honesty, fairness, and respect as key elements of versatility. Those interested in comparing the two concepts can read David Merrill and Roger Reid, *Personal Styles and Effective Performance* (Radnor, Pa.: Chilton Book Company, 1981).

Chapter Nine: Four Steps to Better Relationships

1. Paul Insel and Henry Lindgren, *Too Close for Comfort: The Psychology of Crowding* (Englewood Cliffs, N.J.: Prentice-Hall, 1978), p. 148.
2. Erving Goffmann, *Interaction Ritual: Essays on Face-to-Face Behavior* (New York: Anchor Books, 1967).

Chapter Ten: How to Identify a Person's Style

1. Sir Arthur Conan Doyle, "The Red-Headed League" in *A Treasury of Sherlock Holmes* (Garden City, N.Y.: Hanover House, 1955), pp. 222–223.

Chapter Twelve: Flexing in Special Situations

1. David Bradford and Allan Cohen, *Managing for Excellence: The Guide to Developing High Performance in Contemporary Organizations* (New York: John Wiley & Sons, 1984), p. 262.
2. Graig Nettles and Peter Golenbock, *Balls* (New York: G. P. Putnam, 1984), p. 195.

Chapter Thirteen: Three Keys to Good Relationships

1. F. G. "Buck" Rodgers, *The IBM Way: Insights Into the World's Most Successful Marketing Organization* (New York: Harper & Row, 1986), p. 11.
2. T. S. Eliot, *The Confidential Clerk* (New York: Harcourt, Brace and World, 1954), p. 108.
3. Edgar Schein, *Process Consultation, Volume II, Lessons for Managers and Consultants* (Reading, Mass.: Addison-Wesley, 1987).
4. Roland Bainton, *The Travail of Religious Liberty* (Philadelphia: Westminster Press, 1951), p. 227.

Index

acceptance, 29
acquiescing behavior, 52–53, 55, 56
aggressiveness, 17
Amiables
  acquiescing behavior of, 52–53, 55, 56
  Analyticals flexing to, 174–178
  antidotes to strengths of, 94–96, 97
  backup styles of, 52–53, 55, 56
  characteristics of, 25, 33–38
  conflict avoidance of, 37–38, 94–96
  Drivers flexing to, 147–153
  Expressives flexing to, 154–158
  flexing to Analyticals, 121–126
  flexing to Drivers, 68, 129–134
  flexing to Expressives, 126–129
  style-based clash between, 108, 109,
    134–135
  style flex for, 121–135
Analyticals
  Amiables flexing to, 121–126
  antidotes to strengths of, 92–94, 97
  avoiding behavior of, 53–54, 55
  backup styles of, 53–54, 55, 56
  characteristics of, 24, 30–33
  Drivers flexing to, 142–147
  Expressives flexing to, 72–74, 161–168
  flexing to Amiables, 174–178
  flexing to Drivers, 71, 170–174
  flexing to Expressives, 178–186
  perfectionism of, 30–31, 92–94
  quality orientation of, 92–94
  style-based clash between, 108, 109,
    186–187
  style flex for, 170–187
Aquarian Conspiracy, The (Ferguson), 11
Ash, Mary Kay, and "golden rule management," 111–112
assertiveness, 16–19
  aggressiveness versus, 17
  characteristics of, 18–19
  defined, 16
  identifying another person's level of,
    82–83
  personal level of, 16–18

  submissiveness versus, 18
  success and, 22–23
  see also Drivers; Expressives
attacking behavior, 49–51, 55
autocratic behavior, 51–52, 55, 56, 89–90
avoiding behavior, 53–54, 55

backup styles, 47–61
  acquiescing behavior, 52–53, 55, 56
  of Amiables, 52–53, 55, 56
  of Analyticals, 53–54, 55, 56
  attacking behavior, 49–51, 55
  autocratic behavior, 51–52, 55, 56
  avoiding behavior, 53–54, 55
  damage control with others, 59–61
  damage control with self, 57–58
  described, 48–49
  of Drivers, 51–52, 55, 56
  of Expressives, 49–51, 55, 56
  identification of, 47–61
  of others, 59–61
  primary, 49–54, 55
  secondary, 54–55, 56
  of self, 57–58
  and stress relief, 56–57
behavior
  acquiescing, 52–53, 55, 56
  attacking, 49–51, 55
  autocratic, 51–52, 55, 56, 89–90
  avoiding, 53–54, 55
  components of, 10
  conflict avoidance, 37–38, 94–96
  outer versus inner, *xii*, 81
  perfectionistic, 30–31, 92–94
  predicting probable, 12, 56
  spontaneous, 41, 91–92
  see also assertiveness; responsiveness;
    style flex
Behavioral Inventory, 13–15
  guidelines for, 13–15
  interpreting, 15, 25–26
body language, 10, 87
Bradford, David, 99
Brahmanism, 111

191

Brain/Mind Bulletin, 11
Branden, Nathaniel, 69
Buddhism, 111

Carlyle, Thomas, 43
Carter, Jimmy, 9
Christianity, 111
Cohen, Allan, 99
comfort zone, 11
communication style, 78
    respect in, 112–115
Confidential Clerk, The (Eliot), 113
conflict avoidance, 37–38, 94–96
conformity, style flex versus, 67–69
Confucianism, 111
Conlan, Jock, 115

decision making, in backup mode, 58, 60
DiMaggio, Joe, 21
Dostoyevsky, Fyodor, 67
Drivers
    Amiables flexing to, 68, 129–134
    Analyticals flexing to, 71, 170–174
    antidotes to strengths of, 89–91, 97
    autocratic tendencies of, 51–52, 55, 56,
        89–90
    backup styles of, 51–52, 55, 56
    characteristics of, 24, 43–46
    Expressives flexing to, 158–161
    flexing to Amiables, 147–153
    flexing to Analyticals, 142–147
    flexing to Expressives, 136–142
    forcefulness of, 89–91
    style-based clash between, 108, 153
    style flex for, 136–153
Drucker, Peter, 30

Eckman, Paul, 22–23
Eliot, T. S., 113
Emerson, Ralph Waldo, 49
empowerment, 78
evaluation, in style flex, 76–77
Expressives
    Amiables flexing to, 126–129
    Analyticals flexing to, 178–186
    antidotes to strengths of, 91–92, 93, 97
    attacking behavior of, 49–51, 55
    backup styles of, 49–51, 55, 56
    characteristics of, 25, 38–43
    Drivers flexing to, 136–142
    flexing to Amiables, 154–158
    flexing to Analyticals, 72–74, 161–168
    flexing to Drivers, 158–161
    spontaneity of, 41, 91–92
    style-based clash between, 108, 168–169
    style flex for, 154–169

fairness, 115–116
Feelers, *xi–xii*

Ferguson, Marilyn, 11
flexing, *see* style flex
Ford Motor Company, 65–66
Franklin, Benjamin, 27
Fromm, Erich, 69

Goffmann, Erving, 78
Golden Rule, 110–112
goodwill, 114–115
groups, flexing to, 101–104
Gulliver's Travels (Swift), 114

habits, 11, 22–23
Hand, Learned, 11
Harris, Sydney, 58
Hillel, 110
honesty, 116–117
Howe, Reuel, 67

identification of styles, *see* style identifica-
    tion
implementation, in style flex, 76
inference, observation versus, 81
inner states, *xii*, 81
Intuiters, *xi–xii*
Islam, 111

Jefferson, Thomas, 54
John, Tommy, 101
John XXIII, Pope, 116
Jordan, Hamilton, 9
judgmental mind-set, 29
Jung, Carl, *xi–xii*
just-in-time flex, 78

Kant, Immanuel, 115
Kauffman, Ewing, 111
Kroc, Ray, 60, 70

labels, for styles, 87
Lincoln, Abraham, 116
listening skills, 89–90
Love, John, 70

Man, The Manipulator (Shostrom), 67
managers, flexing to, 99–100
Managing for Excellence (Bradford and
    Cohen), 99
Mandell, Arnold, 9, 11
manipulation, style flex versus, 66–67, 68
manners, 113–114
Marcus Aurelius, 59
Marion Laboratories, 111
Markham, Howard, 71
McDonald's, 60, 70
Mead, Margaret, 29
Merrill, David, *xii*, 9–10, 16, 22
models, 9–11
    see also PeopleStyles

Morgan, J. P., 21
Myers-Briggs model, *xii*

National Football League (NFL), 9
Nettles, Graig, 101
Nixon, Richard M., 44, 55, 108
Notorius, Clifford, 71

observation
    inference versus, 81
    of personal styles, 80–86
opening in parallel, 78
opinion polls, 9
outer behaviors, *xii*

Parker, Dorothy, 114
Pasternak, Boris, 69
patterns, components of, 10–11
Penney, J. C., 111
people skills
    differences as advantages in, 6–7
    relationships and, 5–6
PeopleStyles, 9–11
perfectionism, 30–31, 92–94
Perls, Fritz, 67
personality, 10
Peterson, Donald, 65–66
planning, for style flex, 75–76
Poling, Red, 65–66
predictability, 8–12
    of behavior, 10
    frequency of, 8–10
    habit and, 11
    patterns and, 10–11
    of probable behavior, 12, 56
psychological models, *xi–xii*
Psychological Types (Jung), *xi–xii*

quality orientation, 30–31, 92–94

rapport
    opening in parallel for, 78
    see also style flex
Rather, Dan, 108
Reagan, Ronald, 9
Reid, Roger, 22
relationships, 110–117
    fairness in, 115–116
    Golden Rule and, 110–112
    honesty in, 116–117
    people skills and, 5–6
    respect in, 112–115
respect
    good manners and, 113–114
    goodwill in, 114–115
    importance of, 112–115
responsiveness, 20–22
    characteristics of, 21–22

identifying another person's level of,
    83–84
personal level of, 20–21
success and, 22–23
    see also Amiables; Expressives
rigidity, and style flex, 79

Sandburg, Carl, 71
Schein, Edgar, 114
second nature, 11
Selye, Hans, 48–49
Sensors, *xi–xii*
Shostrom, Everett, 67
Simmons, Grant G., Jr., 65
Simmons Company, 65
Social Style Model, 9–10
    see also PeopleStyles
speaking ratio, 89–90
spontaneity, 41, 91–92
stress
    backup styles and, 47–61
    style flex for, 79
style flex, 66–71, 99–109
    for Amiables, 121–135
    for Analyticals, 170–187
    and antidotes to strengths, 89–98
    as changing your behavior, 69–71
    conformity versus, 67–69
    defined, *xiv*, 99
    difficulties with, 107
    for Drivers, 136–153
    for Expressives, 154–169
    to groups, 101–104
    guidelines for, 77–79
    for important situations, 78
    just-in-time, 78
    to managers, 99–100
    manipulation versus, 66–67, 68
    opening in parallel, 78
    to people with same style, 107–109
    to a person and a task, 104–106
    and rigidity, 79
    steps in, 72–79
    and stress, 79
    to subordinates, 100–101
    as temporary adjustment, 69–71, 77–78
    see also PeopleStyles; *names of specific styles*
style identification
    assertiveness in, 16–19, 22–23, 82–83
    of backup styles, 47–61
    Behavioral Inventory for, 13–15, 25–26
    body language in, 10, 87
    fine-tuning, 85–86
    of group members, 102–103
    labels in, 87
    observation in, 80–86
    of others' style, 74–75, 80–88
    of personal style, 13–15, 25–27, 74–75

style identification (*continued*)
  problems with, 107
  responsiveness in, 20–22, 23, 83–84
  style clues in, 28–46, 81–84, 85
  style defined, 10
  tips for, 86–88
submissiveness, 18
subordinates, flexing to, 100–101
success
  and location on assertiveness/responsive-
    ness scales, 22–23
  people skills and, 5–6
Swift, Jonathan, 114

Taoism, 111
tasks, flexing to people and, 104–106

Thinkers, *xi–xii*
Thomas, Lewis, 69
Thurber, James, 12
Truman, Harry, 32
Turner, Fred, 70
Twain, Mark, 70
Tyler, Robert P., Jr., 65

Washington, George, 116
Watson, Thomas, Jr., 112
Williams, Roger, 116–117
win-win approach, 115–116
Wolf, Warner, 21
words, choice of, 10
Worthington Industries, 111

Zoroastrianism, 111